Thomas Roscoe Rede Stebbing

Essays on Darwinism

Thomas Roscoe Rede Stebbing

Essays on Darwinism

ISBN/EAN: 9783743413399

Manufactured in Europe, USA, Canada, Australia, Japa

Cover: Foto ©Thomas Meinert / pixelio.de

Manufactured and distributed by brebook publishing software (www.brebook.com)

Thomas Roscoe Rede Stebbing

Essays on Darwinism

ESSAYS ON DARWINISM.

BY

THOMAS R. R. STEBBING, M.A.

Late Fellow and Tutor of Worcester College, Oxford.

LONDON:
LONGMANS, GREEN, AND CO.
1871.

[*All rights reserved*]

OXFORD:
BY T. COMBE, M.A., E. B. GARDNER, AND E. PICKARD HALL,
PRINTERS TO THE UNIVERSITY.

PREFACE.

THE opinions of Mr. Darwin have now been for many years before the world. His own book on 'The Origin of Species by means of Natural Selection,' unfolds and supports them with admirable clearness of argument. Far from being an abstruse and tedious work, it carries the reader on with unflagging interest to the close. Observations and experiments, some the most simple, some the most elaborate, notes on natural history, as well from every quarter of the globe as from almost every province of nature, are brought to bear upon the subject without confusion of thought or embarrassment of style. The language flows easily in its calm, temperate, unegotistical course. There is no disguising of objections, no seeking of opponents. There is an evident searching after truth. Of its form or of its shadow the author's mind as evidently retains a bright clear vision, and what he sees he tries to make others see as clearly as he sees it himself. The suspicion and dislike which are aroused in some minds by the very name of Darwinism cannot be retained by those who read Mr. Darwin's own description of his theory and the grounds which slowly led him to adopt it. Few readers can be dull enough to feel no charm at finding the most unlooked-for results deduced from the simplest illustrations, from old familiar facts, from every-day occurrences, or at finding what seem examples of the most special and varied contrivance reconciled to the simplicity of a single general law. Many readers will be inclined to whisper to themselves at many passages, ' we never thought of that before,' ' we never looked at the matter in that light,' ' how curious if after all it should be true,' 'it looks less wicked and silly than we used to think it.' Whether the theory itself be right or wrong, the general effect of the book which describes it can only be to quicken the minds of its readers, to enlarge for them the circle of ideas, to open up before them new lines of thought and enquiry, to let them see the whole face of nature teeming with mysteries and revelations, an inexhaustible vintage for the human reason to gather in.

Such being the character of Mr. Darwin's own Work, the handful of Essays and Letters contained in the present volume, supporting the same views by almost the same arguments, may seem a superfluous contribution to the literature of the question. And so it would be if all who condemn and ridicule Darwinism would be at the pains to study Mr. Darwin's Work. But opinions passed upon it and allusions made to it in common conversation and in popular lectures often testify to nothing except supreme ignorance of its general merits. To judge by such hearsay, one might believe that Mr. Darwin had lived all his life shut up in a dove-cote, and never seen or examined any other living creature than a pigeon. Another estimate will dismiss the whole subject, scathed with indignant laughter, by simply explaining, that, according to this fatuous theory, man is descended from a monkey. Naturally no well-minded persons will consent to be *pithecoid* in origin, whether they know what *pithecoid* means or not ; still less can a theory be accepted as moral and good, according to which, as some will tell you, the giraffe lengthened its neck by a series of stretchings, and the elephant acquired a trunk by continually pulling its own nose. A disinterested advocate will perhaps be allowed to deprecate these burlesque and ignorant representations, and to strip from what is merely vulgar prejudice the guise of magnanimity and fine feeling. The range of topics embraced in the present volume, however feebly handled, and however inaccurate that handling may in some points prove to be, should at least teach those who are willing to learn, that the whole subject is a great one, and worthy of attention, claiming earnest thought and varied learning to decide upon it in all its bearings; it cannot be disposed of by caricaturing; it cannot be settled in deference to any religious prepossession; it must be examined with open eyes, and with the full candour of mind which great subjects demand, and which great subjects nobly repay.

Some of the following papers treat of matters on which no man of scientific education can be supposed at the present day to retain even a vestige of doubt. But thousands of persons, whom in ordinary courtesy we must call well-educated, although they know nothing of science, hold opinions on the Flood and the age of the world as irreconcileable with the best-approved scientific conclusions as they are with the Darwinian Theory. In appealing to the judgment of such persons, as well as in considering the measure of his own powers, the present writer has thought it expedient to confine himself, for the most part, to the clearest and simplest arguments, leaving on one side the subtle and intricate.

The letters collected at the end of the volume may be looked on as short essays of a somewhat informal character. The apology for reprinting them is this, that whereas in a regular essay the writer assumes his own standpoint, and may be suspected of ignoring the vantage-ground of his opponents, in replying to a correspondent he must, at least to some extent, follow the lead of an antagonist, and fight, if he fights at all, on the field which another has chosen.

As I cannot reprint the various able compositions which I have attempted to answer, it will be fair, to one at least of the writers, to remark that I have personal reason to know that he still retains the opinions of which I attempted to disabuse him. He contrives to reconcile this obduracy to his own intelligence by laying stress on the candid admission made by Darwinians, that the Theory of Development is for the present that which they call it,—a Theory, and not a demonstration. No one pretends to answer fully every objection that has been urged against the Theory. The evidence is as yet incomplete. By its very nature it must perhaps always to some extent remain so. The proof depends in part upon analogy, which leads to conclusions possible or probable, rather than to what is demonstrably certain. But the advocates of the Theory, remembering Bishop Butler's maxim, that 'to us probability is the very guide of life,' endeavour to maintain that their opinions have far more than that minimum of preponderance which, in Butler's view, not only justifies, but imperiously exacts, the adhesion of reasonable beings.

THOMAS R. R. STEBBING.

Torquay, Feb. 6, 1871.

CONTENTS.

	PAGE
DARWINISM [1]	3
THE NOACHIAN FLOOD [1]	34
INSTINCT AND REASON [2]	62
HUMAN NATURE AND BRUTE NATURE	82
THE LAPSE OF TIME [1]	93
NOTE ON THE HYPOTHESIS OF SPONTANEOUS GENERATION [1]	126
IMPERFECTION OF THE GEOLOGICAL RECORD [1]	133
DARWINISM: THE NOACHIAN FLOOD	147
DARWINISM: SCIENCE AND RELIGION	152
DARWINISM, AND THE FIRST VERTEBRATE	156
THE FIRST VERTEBRATE, AND THE BEGINNING OF REASON	160
OYSTERS OF THE CHALK, AND THE THEORY OF DEVELOPMENT	165
THE MATHEMATICAL TEST OF NATURAL SELECTION	168
THE GENESIS OF SPECIES	173
INDEX	181

[1] These papers were read at various dates between February 1869 and January 1871, before the Torquay Natural History Society.
[2] Read before the Devonshire Association, July 1870.

NOTES to pp. 13 and 34.

It has been kindly pointed out to me by Mr. James Parker of Oxford that there is an error in Mr. Darwin's calculation reproduced in page 13 of this volume. Upon the data supplied, the increase in the number of elephants there mentioned would require 750 years instead of 500. The further increase calculated in the same page, would in like manner require seven or eight additional centuries instead of five.

Mr. Parker also suggests that the expressions in page 34, 'taken for granted,' 'taught for centuries,' seem to ignore Bishop Stillingfleet and other writers of his time, who saw good reason for believing the Flood in the days of Noah not to have been universal. I am glad to explain that I did not by any means intend to imply that there were no exceptions to the general state of opinion, for I am well aware that there are at the present day some schools, a few nurseries, and even one or two pulpits, into which the truth on this point has been allowed to penetrate.

DARWINISM.

DARWINISM.

THE object of this lecture is to explain, with as much simplicity as possible, the opinions of Darwin on the chain of secondary causes which has resulted in the wonderful structures known to us as living creatures, and including, in an almost infinite variety, lichen and moss, mite and mildew, grass and flower and branching tree; mollusk and reptile and fish; the swan, the petrel, the ostrich and the eagle; the cunning ape; the faithful hound; the elephant, sagacious and mindful of insults; the lion, capable of generosity; the horse, patient of labours and eager for victory; and, along with a multitude of others diversely qualified, One, without doubt partaking of the animal nature that lives and dies, yet seeming to partake of something beyond it, seeming to be distinguished from all the rest by its postures, by its laughing, by its cooking its food, by its articulate language, by its powers of reasoning; and yet linked and united to its inferiors by a multitude of affinities and sympathies, resemblances of form and nature, and by the very details of its superiority. So ran the Pagan legend that Providence had compacted man's moral nature out of particles taken from each of the lower animals, giving him the wisdom of the serpent and the fiery courage of the lion[1]. To this sense of an intimate union between man and the rest of the animate creation have the writers of fables in all ages appealed, while imparting their lessons of prudence and virtue under the guise of transactions between birds and beasts and trees of the forest.

It is well known that after the discovery of almost every great truth a sort of feeling or instinct of it can be traced back in obscure hints, in chance expressions, in vague guesses, in flights of imagination, so that people very soon begin to fancy that they have all along understood and maintained the very theory, which, on its first appearance, they violently rejected as something false and even vicious. Darwinism has this characteristic of truth, that it has often been obscurely anticipated. It has this other characteristic, that its fiercest opponents have already begun insensibly to adopt its conclusions, and to speak its language, to opine, even, that the credit of its promulgation belongs to themselves.

In Mr. Darwin's own historical sketch of the rise and progress of his doctrine, he does full justice to those who have preceded and who have worked with him in bringing it to light and in establishing its foundations. The opinion that species originate, not by successive miraculous interpositions or acts of creation, but by

---

[1] Horace, Odes, I. xvi. 13 :—
  Fertur Prometheus addere principi
  Limo coactus particulam undique
  Desectam, et insani leonis
   Vim stomacho apposuisse nostro.

birth, was held as far back as 1794–5, by four men of distinguished genius, by Lamarck, by Mr. Darwin's own grandfather, Dr. Erasmus Darwin, by Geoffroy Saint Hilaire, and by the poet Goethe. In the present day, Mr. Wallace, Mr. Herbert Spencer, the great zoologist Van Baer, and others, independently of Mr. Darwin, seem to have come more or less to the same conclusions, which have been warmly espoused and powerfully vindicated by Dr. Hooker, Professor Huxley, and Sir Charles Lyell. I mention these names because it seems to be their due, and not for the sake of giving weight to any argument because of the scientific renown of its advocates; there are names, it may be, equally distinguished on the opposite side. But one thing ought to be observed, that the progress of scientific enquiry has achieved so much during the last hundred years that the opinions of the older Naturalists have an importance when they agree with modern conclusions, which they cannot have when they differ from them, unless it can be shown that the observations, the experiments, the discoveries of late years had all been made by, or were known to, the earlier enquirers. For those, however, who think the opinions of a past generation of necessity more trustworthy than those of the present, Sir Charles Lyell has done well to point out that Linnæus himself looked forward to a time when it should be proved that in botany, at least, all species of a genus had descended from the same mother [1].

This is precisely Mr. Darwin's opinion on the origin

[1] Lyell, 'Principles of Geology,' vol. ii. p. 324. Tenth Edition.

of species at large. He applies it to the animal as well as to the vegetable kingdom. He extends it by considering genera themselves as species of the orders which contain them, and orders as species of the great classes to which they as orders respectively belong. In a word, he considers that all living forms whatsoever are descended from a very few original ancestors of the simplest type, and that this primæval group itself had, probably, a common parentage. Wildly improbable, ludicrously absurd, degrading to humanity, and irreligious, no doubt this hypothesis has appeared to many, and will continue so to appear till it has been studied with attention, and studied without prejudice. To rescue it from the prejudice which would make it in the eyes of some a pernicious and forbidden study, is the hope which underlies the object of the present lecture.

Round Nelson's Column in Trafalgar Square there are four colossal statue lions, the conception of a great artist. They look unnatural, not because of their size, or their position, or the material of which they are made, but because they are all so exactly alike; and exact likenesses are scarcely ever found in animate nature, unless it be among the very simplest organisms. When we speak of a striking likeness between two human beings, we evidently imply that a high degree of similarity is uncommon, and, therefore, noteworthy. What is true of even the most highly organized animals, is true, as far as observation goes, of all below them. Horses, dogs, sheep, kine, afford familiar illustrations of this principle. To the uneducated eye, individual differences may be totally unapparent, which are yet perfectly conspicuous to the trainer, the huntsman, the shepherd, and the drover. Wild creatures know their mates; wild herds select their leaders; the bee and the ant are capable of distinguishing the various individuals of their own communities, for strangers of the very self-same species with themselves they repel or destroy[1]. As each creature is, in numberless cases, the offspring of two unlike parents, it cannot be an exact copy of either, and the influences of the two parents may be combined in various proportions in each of the offspring; but the parents themselves are continually changing, with the variations of age and food and climate, so that the very rule of resemblance between the producers and the produced will entail another rule of unlikeness between the several members of an offspring not born all at once.

It is a fact, which cannot be denied, that in numberless instances the young of a creature differ more or less from the parents and likewise among themselves. Why it should be so has been in part explained. This is the *Variability*, without which Natural Selection could never have been thought of, because without differences there would have been nothing to select. But this Variability being granted, the Darwinian theory becomes possible — becomes quite capable of referring back the elephant and the pig, for instance, to the same ancestry. The difference between progenitors and

[1] Darwin, 'Animals and Plants under Domestication,' vol. ii. p. 251.

their immediate offspring are, it is true, comparatively slight. It would, indeed, be a prodigious birth if one family contained at once a young monkey, a little pig, a big donkey, and a great goose; but it is obviously possible that any amount of unlikeness may be found between the descendants of common ancestors, if we are not confined to the differences of a single generation, but are allowed to multiply them through as many thousands as we require. Say that two race-courses differ in length by one yard; multiply that difference 1760 times and they will then differ by a whole mile. If, on leaving this Lecture-room, you found the trees—which half-an-hour ago were bare and leafless—clothed with summer verdure, your gardens blooming with a wealth of roses, your orchards laden with autumnal fruits, you would scarcely credit your senses; and yet, when the requisite number of half-hours, reckoned by days and months, shall have elapsed, you will greet these wonderful changes as perfectly natural and nothing to be wondered at. In a dissolving view that is well managed, Alpine peak and glacier-pass melt imperceptibly into some tall cathedral and sunshiny marketplace. The two scenes are wholly unlike, and yet it is contrived that at no moment should the passage from one to the other be discernibly abrupt. Is it not possible then to conceive that through an immense multitude of generations the form of an ape might be derived from the form of a fish? We do not mean to say that this has actually happened, but supposing the descendant of the fish to vary continuously in the direction of the ape-like form, the result would be intelligible enough. What, then, is there to determine variation in any particular direction, and what limits are there, if any, to the system of interminable change which the principle of variation seems to involve?

Of course it is understood that the general mass of characters or qualities belonging to any creature are inherited by one generation from its immediate ancestors and transmitted to its immediate descendants, so that for a long period there would be a large number of individuals in the world united into a group by common characters, which according to their supposed importance we might call specific or generic. But besides this, there is the very curious principle of *Reversion* to be taken into account, as largely conducing to the comparative permanence of species. In Norway, I believe, when the father's name is Jack, and the son's name is Tom, Tom is called Tom Jackson, and Tom is in the habit of giving his own eldest son the grandfather's name, and then Tom Jackson's son is called Jack Tomson. Now, in the same way, in nature it not unfrequently happens that when a long-nosed man is father of a short-nosed son, the son of the short-nosed man inherits by reversion the more elongated feature of his grandsire. Under certain conditions, which however greatly limit it, the operation of this principle of Reversion may extend, so far as we know, to any quality whatever after an interval of any number of generations. The tendency, therefore, is to the permanence of species, and yet, as will be shown in the sequel, it has furnished Mr. Darwin with an additional argument to prove that species are not permanent. It must be borne in mind that when a character reverts from a very distant ancestor, the creature which inherits it will have numerous other qualities, all probably more or less differing from those originally united to the reversionary character; just as if, in the School of Art, a picture by Raffaelle were shown to fifty pupils, and when it had been copied by the first, the second pupil were to make a copy of the copy, and so on to the end, each of the copies would no doubt differ more and more from the original, and yet in the very last, by the help of memory or sympathetic genius, there might be some beauty not to be found in any of the others, recalling the hand of the great master; while it is true, that if the sketch were something exceedingly simple, the fiftieth copy, and all the intermediate ones, might be almost exactly like the original; and so in nature, exceedingly simple organisms are seemingly reproduced for almost endless generations with no change, or scarcely any.

If it be true that all living creatures on this earth spring from a very few, extremely simple, original germs of life, we have to explain how it is that now there is an enormous variety of highly organised creatures, and at the same time some of extreme simplicity. For, if the simplest forms are permanent, how can the more complex be derived from them? On the other hand, if the simplest forms vary, how is it that we find, as we do, the very earliest known form of life still living at the present day? The solution is easy to suggest, that the offspring of very simple forms are sometimes exactly like their parents, and sometimes not exactly like. From what has been said above of Inheritance and Variation, this is in the highest degree probable, and, this being admitted, it will follow that according to circumstances the progeny that are like their parents, or those that are unlike, will have the best of it. Why this follows will now have to be explained.

All over the surface of our globe there is *a struggle for life* going on. The instinct of self-preservation is probably stronger than any other, so that we may rely upon it that the creatures of every race will strive to preserve their own existence, if need be, at the expense of that of others. It may be horrible to the sentimentalist, but it is true; and remember that man as well as the tiger is a carnivorous mammal. There is no beast or bird of prey that can be compared with man for his ravaging, destructive, butchering, remorseless dissipation of other forms of life, to preserve his own existence and make it comfortable. He secures his gluttony from famine, as far as he can, by being omnivorous. Moss and fungus, grass and herb, leaf and flower and stem and fruit, all alike find a grave in man. The lion and the flea are the victims of his fear; many a harmless snake and toad of his antipathy; the otter and the fox die for his sport; the ostrich and the ermine for his vanity. For his food, like a wolf, he slays the harmless sheep; like a hawk, he pounces on the innocent chicken; like a wily panther, surprises the antlered stag; devours fish like a shark; spreads nets for his prey like a spider; and in some instances acquires a well-developed taste for the flesh of his fellow-man. Practically with all living animals, the first consideration is food. If all living animals could obtain abundance of pleasant and suitable food without preying on one another, the scene of war which Nature presents would perhaps in a great measure disappear. Yet this warfare is as conspicuous in the vegetable as it is in the animal kingdom. There is a certain amount of nourishment in a given piece of ground, and for that nourishment the plants upon it will compete, some thriving and multiplying to the hindrance and destruction of the others. Here again, if the surface of the globe supplied nutriment for all its plants, there would be at least no need for this destructive competition.

And how is it that this wide, wide world does not supply food enough for all the vegetable forms that make an effort to live upon it? The answer to this curious question has long been known, though not sufficiently attended to. It would not be fair to say that Nature is stingy in her supplies of food, but rather that she is too generously prolific of forms of life. For, take the supposition that all living creatures, whether animal or vegetable, were shielded from all enemies and influences at present hurtful to them, and let us see to what it would bring us. A single grain of wheat produces an ear containing ten, twenty, or some larger number of grains. But if the ear contained only two grains, still, at that rate of increase, a single grain would in thirty years be represented by more than a thousand millions of grains [1]. What, then, would be the position of the world, if, starting with a thousand millions of grains, this rate of increase were allowed to continue unchecked, not for thirty years, but for three thousand? But Mr. Darwin has calculated in regard to the elephant, which is reckoned the slowest breeder of all known animals, that, according to the very lowest probable rate of natural increase, a single pair would in five hundred years have a progeny of fifteen million living elephants [2]. Now fancy an island like our own, only in a climate suitable to elephants, into which a couple should have found their way a thousand years back. At the end of five hundred years, if all that were born were enabled to breed unchecked, there would be at least fifteen millions of their huge descendants stalking about the land; but, at the end of five hundred years more, there would be one hundred and twelve millions of millions of elephants. Goodness! What a stupendous menagerie! What a zoological garden! What a prospect at the end of the next five hundred years! And all this time, remember, according to our sentimental, philanthropic, philelephantine, nature-improving scheme, the men and women, the donkeys with a soul above thistles, the thistles no longer toothsome to donkeys, the mice, the rats, the cats, the oaks, the cabbages, the toadstools, would have

[1] 1,073,741,824 grains.
[2] 'On the Origin of Species,' p. 74. Fourth Edition.

been multiplying, not in the same proportion as the elephants, but very much more rapidly. The great desideratum would be standing room. The back of an elephant, or the branch of an oak, would no doubt command an enormous rent, and a right of way across the heads of your neighbours would be religiously guarded by the law of the land. Nor would the position of affairs be better in the surrounding sea; for while these elephants have been computed to breed at the rate of two young ones in thirty years, a single codfish has been found to produce in one year more than six millions of eggs, and there are other creatures infinitely more prolific [1].

You see, then, that the struggle for existence is an absolute necessity; and out of this all-essential strife springs what has been well called Natural Selection. What is meant by this will more easily be understood by looking first at Artificial Selection, which has been practised by man, sometimes consciously, and oftener unconsciously, in the process of domesticating a great number of plants and animals. Dogs, sheep, bulls, pigs, horses, fowls, pigeons, cabbages, and other culinary vegetables, strawberries, and all manner of edible fruits, together with gay-coloured, curiously-formed, sweetly-perfumed garden-flowers innumerable, have been, and are still being, subjected to man's selection. That the wonderful changes which occur are indeed due to man's repeated choice of the varieties which suit his purposes,

[1] Darwin, 'Animals and Plants under Domestication,' vol. ii. p. 379.

is clear from this, that all the remarkable changes have taken place in those particular qualities which man has valued, leaving the other qualities comparatively unaltered. Let it be speed, size, taste, colour, form, temper, the coat, the feathers, the flesh, the muscular strength, the powers of endurance; in a vegetable, let it be the root, the stem, the leaf, the flower, the fruit, the seed, let it be what it will that is of value, that part and that character have been in each case most highly developed. To take a few examples: You are fond of peas, and you sow in your garden what your seedsman tells you are the finest new varieties; you like strawberries, you admire roses, you fancy a good cabbage, you are particular about having a mealy potato; so in each case you plant what you understand to be the best new kinds. What will you say if it turns out that the roses have improved in their roots but not in the bloom, and the potatoes in the bloom but not in their tubers; that the strawberries have remarkably fine leaves but very small fruit; that the peas and the cabbages have indeed enormous stems, while the seed of the one and the leaf of the other are insignificant in size and tasteless to the palate? So, too, if you purchase a race-horse and a pig from the most noted breeders of those animals, will you not be disgusted if it turns out that the horse has a remarkable propensity for fattening, while the pig is distinguished by nothing but its extreme fleetness of foot? These disappointments do not occur, because the variations of domesticated plants and animals are selected by competent persons. Were strawberry-leaves of as much importance in horticulture as they are in heraldry, many fine varieties would soon be exhibited. As soon as the most minute tendency to vary in any particular direction has been descried in any living creature, the fancier can exaggerate the difference to an extent inconceivable to the inexperienced. As a popular illustration of this we may take the Big Gooseberry, which fills so large a space in the newspapers when Parliament is prorogued. A gooseberry has been grown weighing more than 37 pennyweights—that is, nearly two ounces[1]. But mere size is not a fair test of the extreme plasticity of living organisms. You may have your trees growing stiffly upright, or with pendulous branches and prostrate stems; you may have your cattle long-horned, short-horned, or with no horns at all; your rabbits straight-eared or lop-eared; your fowls with every variety of comb and crest and wattles and plumage; and your pigeons pretty well at discretion. A type is prefigured, and the fancier produces it; and what is done for amusement with pigeons, is done for food, for profit, for the good of mankind at large, by the grower of corn, by the breeder of sheep, by all the wise produce-masters of the world[2].

Such is Artificial Selection; but man is after all but one of Nature's works, and one of her numerous agents.

---

[1] 37 dwts. 7 grs., or 895 grs., between seven and eight times the size of the wild fruit. See 'Animals and Plants under Domestication,' vol. i. p. 356.

[2] Darwin, 'Animals and Plants under Domestication,' passim.

All that he does, however miraculous it may seem, can only be done under her conditions, and by the means which she supplies. In Artificial Selection man does but take advantage of the natural laws of Inheritance and Variation, and while he is seeking by means of these to produce one alteration, Nature herself is producing perhaps a hundred others. For, by the law of *Correlation,* when one part changes, some other or others almost inevitably change with it. Whether it be shortening the beak of a pigeon or lengthening the neck of a giraffe that is in question, Nature takes care, along with the change, to make other adaptations of the structure in the creature's interest under its altered circumstances. Surely, the working of this principle of Correlation indicates a far-sighted Providence of the results, the disastrous monstrosities, that would otherwise have sprung from the law of Variation.

Man's efforts are considerably limited, moreover, by the law of Reversion. Now, supposing many differing species to be descended, as we maintain, from common ancestors, what ought to be the observable effects of this law? Evidently, we should expect the character of one species now and then to appear in species allied to it, or species of kindred origin to vary in the same manner. In accordance with such an expectation, we find the horse and the ass sometimes assuming the stripes of the quagga and the zebra; certain varieties of the pigeon, the fowl, the turkey, the canary-bird, the duck, and the goose, all have top-knots or reversed feathers on their heads; one kind of melon resembles a cucumber in everything but taste; there are purple-leaved varieties of the beech and the hazel; and a great multitude of plants sometimes exhibit their leaves cut, blotched, and variegated [1].

Now, from the working of Nature under, as it were, man's guidance, we pass to the working of Nature when left to her own discretion. The work of Natural Selection is a very slow and secret work; the slowness of it veils the movement. As with the hour-hand of a tiny watch travelling but an inch in a day, there is progress which you cannot discern, there is change that can be marked and registered at intervals, though each successive moment and each successive movement seem to leave things exactly as they were. You have heard of the Greek simpleton who had been told that a raven lived three hundred years, and so bought one to see. We might live three thousand years instead of three hundred without being able to prove the theory of Natural Selection by actual observing. But when a group of most important observed facts can be explained consistently by this theory, and by none other, while no fact has been brought forward to make it inadmissible, it ought to be accepted till some theory can be produced equally unimpeachable and explanatory of a larger group of facts.

Qualities are inherited; but with this peculiarity, that very generally, and sometimes of necessity, the inheritor comes into possession of the inherited quality at the same period of life at which it was acquired by the

[1] 'Animals and Plants under Domestication,' vol. ii. pp. 348-351.

parent. As, for instance, the child of a gouty father, though it may be destined in old age to inherit the disease, is not born with the gout, any more than a calf is born with horns, or a cherry-tree produced covered with cherries. In the life of every creature there is not merely growth, but development. At every stage of life it is possible for some quality acquired by variation to be fixed by Natural Selection. But in the embryonic and earliest stages of development, variation is least likely to be of service to any creature. Such variations, therefore, will less often be selected than others, and if it be true that many species have a common ancestry, then it ought to be found that in their embryonic and earliest stages they resemble one another. This is precisely what we do find. Plants, the most remote in appearance and properties when full grown, differ but slightly in their cotyledons: the difference between the egg of a nightingale and the egg of an ostrich bears no proportion to the dissimilarity between the two birds when fully developed; nor by comparing the roe of a herring with the roe of a salmon could you possibly guess, before experience, how the full-grown fish would differ. But in the life of every human being there is a stage of development, at which the most sagacious physician could not distinguish him from the embryo of a snake, a lizard, a bird, or an ape[1].

[1] An important caution may here be quoted from Mr. Herbert Spencer. 'An impression,' he says, ' has been given by those who have popularized the sentiments of Embryologists, that, during its development, each higher organism passes through stages in which it resembles the adult forms of lower organisms—that the embryo of a man is at one

Now, if the simplest embryonic forms of life were the progenitors of all existing forms, this is intelligible; but how else can it be explained?

But, again, if species do not vary, how comes it that those living at the present day are for the most part not to be found among the fossil creatures of the ancient rocks? Well, some will tell you there have been many distinct creations, following after many catastrophes potent to destroy all the previous inhabitants of the globe. Well, I will answer, if you rest on Scripture, that view has no basis in Scripture, but if you do not rest on Scripture, it certainly has no scientific foundation, for though the crust of the globe has been made what it is almost exclusively by the action of fire and water, the effect of any sudden convulsions has been a mere nothing as compared with the results from the steady, slow-going, ceaselessly-operating forces of those two agents. Besides, when you look back through the rocks of different ages, not only do you find some forms the same in all, which testifies to the permanent unity of the living creation, but in those forms which differ, you find the differences increasing the further you go back, and some forms you find which have no modern representatives, forms, that is, which have been beaten in the struggle for existence.

time like a fish, and at another time like a reptile. This is not the fact. The fact established is, that up to a certain point the embryos of a man and a fish continue similar, and that then differences begin to appear and increase—the one embryo approaching more and more towards the form of a fish; the other diverging from it more and more. And so with the resemblances to the more advanced types.'—*Principles of Biology*, vol. i. p. 143.

Travel over the globe, and every country will present you with some new species; distant rivers, distant islands, in the ocean shallows separated by great deeps, the opposite sides of a continent, the twin sides of a mountain chain, the foot, the spur, the knee, the breast, the snow-clad head of an Alpine range, will all present you with their own peculiar forms of life. And how came they there? Created, some will say, *in* those regions and *for* those regions, because of their special adaptation to them. Yet, since the globe has been inhabited, vast tracts of it have changed their climates from tropical heat to frozen gloom, and again, yielded the thick-ribbed ice to genial suns and fragrant zephyrs. Unhappy species, the creatures of a fixed idea, created for the temperate meridian of Devonshire, and condemned by the thoughtlessness of nature, to pass their lives in a climate like that of Nova Zembla!

But further, had each species been assigned to its station as some suppose, by a single act of creation, is it not reasonable, does not reverence require us to expect, that each species would have been best off in its own station? But this is not the case. On the contrary, imported species of plants and animals often thrive prodigiously in their new *habitat*, and over-run it.

Once more, we find in numberless plants and animals rudimentary organs that are of no use to the possessors, —mammæ, that give no milk; pistils, in male florets; in insects wings too small for flight, and soldered to the wing cases; the fifth toe in the hind-foot of the dog; the spur of the hen; the wing of the Apteryx; and the stunted, ineffectual, but ever-present tail in our noble selves.

On the old theory of creation, in face of these facts, we cannot save the admired doctrine that nature does nothing in vain; but on the Darwinian theory of creation, that doctrine still holds good, and wisdom is still justified by all her productions; for Natural Selection works only for the good of a species; it does not work in vain, or waste its efforts in getting rid of any organ simply because it is useless, so long as it is not injurious; it leaves it as it was and where it was, a germ, a capacity, perhaps, in the future, to be re-developed or fitted for a new purpose.

Here we have incidentally touched upon what seems to be morally the grandest part of the whole theory, an even sublime explanation, as far as it goes, of that small fraction which we see in terrestrial life of the great and manifold works of God. We noted above that it is to death, a necessity much hated, much maligned, that we owe the possibility of our own birth and standing-room on the face of the globe; but the theory of Natural Selection makes it further clear that the causes of death which we most dread and think evil of—war and famine and pestilence—are tending continually to improve the races of living creatures. On the whole, the wisest, the strongest, the healthiest survive to propagate their species. In the long run, prudence, courage, and temperance prevail, and their owners become the parents of the later generations.

When the competition for life becomes severe, as to

every race of creatures, man included, it does at times become, the smallest advantageous variation will give its possessor a superior chance of surviving, while the smallest that is disadvantageous will diminish the chance. Take the apposite instance of a number of quadrupeds incapable of climbing, supported by browsing on the leaves of trees during a dearth of other suitable food. When the lower leaves within the general reach were exhausted, the famine still continuing, those animals alone would survive which, by some peculiarity, could reach the higher leaves. In this way, those that could spring best, those that could assume even a climbing posture, those endowed with the longest legs, snouts, or necks, would be selected. In some such a way, then, we can conceive the jumping powers of the kangaroo and the antelope, the climbing powers of the bear and the cat, the trunk of the elephant, and the long neck of the giraffe to have been evolved by natural selection. The keen scent of the hound, the sharp eye of the lynx, the gay colours of the butterfly, the splendid plumage of the bird of Paradise, are all easy to account for on this principle of natural selection. So, too, are the dull colours of many female birds, to whom obscurity is useful in protecting their young; so, too, the almost blindness of the mole, which works in the dark, and to which an instrument at once delicate and useless, would entail the risk of positive injury.

The principle explains what no other hypothesis has ever done, not only Nature's perfection, which, in the hour of ease, we are ready to believe in, but what has hitherto been a much greater puzzle to those who knew of its existence, Nature's imperfection. The whole creation is in constant travail to bring forth something better than its present best. The products of man's reason are not, you will readily admit, always perfect, and yet man's reason is a part of the creation, and of nature's work. The waste of life is prodigious, if such a term is applicable to the circumstance that often millions of spores are produced in order that half a dozen plants may grow; millions of eggs in the roe of a fish, in order that the parents may be represented by three or four individuals. The bee defends itself by its sting, but its weapon of defence is fatal to itself. Were a merchant habitually to send five or six million articles of merchandize across the Atlantic on the bare possibility that five or six articles out of the number might reach their destination; or, were a father to arm his son with a weapon on the presumption that the first time he used it, it would cost him his life; you would think the man mad, not wise. Yet, if the astonishing fecundity of the braken, the mushroom, and the codfish, if the sting of the bee with its backward serratures, be the products of direct creation, the analogy is somewhat telling. How different, on the other hand, must our judgment be of those contrivances, when we trace them to the simple, primary, beneficent law of natural selection, working always steadily for the good of each species, and so working, that we may feel tolerably sure that when any species dies out and disappears, it has been replaced by something better. For by this law, we see that fertility itself is a character which will be selected as tending to the preservation of a species, and that many creatures must have acquired the power of what looks like wasteful reproduction in the long-continued struggle for existence. We can see, too, how in that same struggle, it may have proved expedient for a creature to be armed with a weapon capable of inspiring terror, yet so contrived that its possessor should, of necessity, be peaceful towards its neighbours. True, this might have been done by a single act of creation, but why, then, was it not done also in the case of the mosquito, the wasp, and the hornet?

On the theory of sudden creation, how can we account in any but an arbitrary manner, for the innumerable cases in which slight differences separate various species; for the confused neutral ground between different classes, as where, for example, a creature seems half animal half plant; for the isolation of many forms from the stations they are admirably fitted to occupy; for the fact that many creatures are hideous, weak, timid, violent, and venomous; for the imperfection of an instinct in one species found perfected in another, which Mr. Darwin exemplifies by comparing the cells of the humble-bee, the *melipona domestica* of Mexico, and the hive-bee, ranging from great simplicity to an extreme perfection[1]?

---

[1] 'Origin of Species,' p. 270. Mr. Darwin shows how the hexagonal cells of the hive-bee can have arisen from the simple cylindrical form, by bringing the cylinders sufficiently near together, so that their outlines, if completed, would intersect.

The humble-bee makes separate and very irregular rounded cells.

The *melipona domestica* makes cells that are nearly spherical, but

But the principle of natural selection offers a solution to every one of these enigmas. It embraces all the various phases of life of the ancient world as well as the modern, and gives a key to the whole grand uninterrupted plan. It carries back the mind to a period when the earth was destitute of life; when yet, as it were, the thought in the Divine mind was still unspoken, that of one, and that as good as dead, should spring seed like the sand which is upon the sea-shore for multitude. Then it came to pass that the dust of the earth was called into life by the Life-Giver, and received the strange command and the mysterious power to multiply, and to replenish the earth. As soon as living creatures multiplied to any great extent, they would spread themselves into different lands and seas and climates; they would find different sources of nourishment, and then variation would come into play, and close upon variation would follow selection, not of necessity destroying the old forms, but establishing new ones, because in some stations the form that had not varied might thrive best, in others the variety would have an advantage[1]. As time went on, through the constant changes that the surface of the globe is undergoing, one variety would be isolated from another, and in such an isolation the differences would increase. And the more a species

---

too near together for the spheres to be complete, flat walls of wax being built where they tend to intersect.

A little extra regularity, advantageous for the saving of wax and labour, would produce the symmetrical comb of the hive-bee with its two layers of hexagonal prisms.

[1] See 'Principles of Biology,' vol. i. pp. 428-431.

varied, the more fitted it might become for some *habitat*, from which it was completely cut off by a chain of mountains, a rapid river, or a deep sea. As the competition became more intense, variations would become more and more valuable, enabling creatures to occupy positions before untenable, ocean-depths, sandy shores, holes in rocks, fresh-water lakes, tops of mountains, branches of trees, the bodies of other living beings. Some would be taught by necessity and enabled by favourable variations to prey, as well as take up their abode, on other creatures. And as the strife became more and more urgent, all sorts of qualities that from our point of view may seem noxious and degrading might prove of the highest service and advantage to their own possessors. Plants with sharp thorns and envenomed hairs, poisonous snakes, trichinæ and other parasites horrible to man, would find their advantage at our cost, or by unparalleled fertility would defy all efforts to extirpate them. Some species would profit by minuteness, others by size; others, in various ways, by talons, beak, thread-like tongue, prehensile tail, or furry coat; and, just as men are said to go through fire and water for the sake of money, so for the sake of preservation, no habit, no locality would be too uncongenial for a species to develope adaptation thereunto. And, accordingly, we find that the water-ouzel, which is a species of thrush, subsists entirely by diving; there is a tree-climbing lobster in the Mauritius; there are fishes which ramble about on the land, and one fish, the *anabas scandens*, can climb eight or ten feet up the trunk of a palm[1].

The choice of food, the choice of habitation, the construction of dwelling-places for themselves or their offspring, methods of defence, methods of attack, are variously carried out by myriads of species. The processes employed, in man we call for the most part rational; in the lower animals we call them instinctive; but there are processes employed for these self-same objects by vegetables as well as by men. For plants, in one sense stationary, travel towards water by their roots, towards light by their branches; they assimilate the elements of nutriment that suit them, rejecting others. The Sensitive plant shrinks from the touch, Venus's fly-trap closes round unwary insects and destroys them. Tendrils fasten on the supports that are offered them. Trees keep in their delicate blossoms till the weather is genial. Many a corolla folds carefully round stamens and pistils when the chilly twilight approaches.

Pass from proceedings like these to the swimming movements of a beheaded Dytiscus[2], and other reflex actions in animals, to the food-seeking movements of the tentaculæ of the Hydra or fresh-water Polype, which

---

[1] 'Origin of Species,' p. 213; 'Principles of Biology,' vol. i. pp. 392, 394. The walking-fishes of India and the mud-fishes of Ceylon and New Zealand are described in an interesting article by Dr. Day of Torquay, in 'All the Year Round' for June 11th, 1870. Dr. Day seems to think the climbing powers of the *anabas scandens* less satisfactorily attested than other attributes of these extraordinary groups.

[2] Carpenter. 'Animal Physiology,' chap. 14.

hover doubtfully between reflex and instinctive action: go forward through the innumerable gradations of instinct till you come, for instance, to the spider, weaving its symmetrical web, rushing out of its lair to seize the prey when the web is shaken lightly, but keeping itself close from a too dangerous foe when the web is vehemently shaken. Examine the nest of the Mygale (the trap-door spider) lined with silken tapestry, furnished with a door on a silken hinge, which it covers above with materials like the surrounding soil, and holds from beneath against an intruder, by applying its claws to the most advantageous point, the point most distant from the hinge: consider the little Sylvia Sutoria, or tailor-bird, which draws filaments of cotton from the cotton-plant, and sews leaves together with its beak and feet to form a nest; go to the huts and river-dams of the beaver; attend a conclave of rooks judging an offender; look into the hive of the hive-bee; observe the conscious vanity of the peacock; preach liberty to the slave-making ants; watch the sagacious ways of dogs and horses; and then lastly see if it be possible to resist the conclusion that, were all forms that ever existed, from the earliest geological times to our own, present before us in the order of their genealogies, we should see them to be the members of a single family, now, indeed, immensely divergent, yet all united by some affinity or affinities, whether dimly or conspicuously shown.

How strangely men and beasts are united by similarity of blood and fibre! How strangely fishes, birds, and mammals by the likeness of the vertebrate skeleton! How strangely plants and animals by the phenomena of generation, not only in the union of the sexes, but also in (*agamogenesis*) or asexual reproduction! Need we wonder at community of origin between a coral and a cactus, a whale and a sloth, a wolf and a Shylock, when we find that a lady's silken tresses, the bristles of a boar, the quill of the porcupine, the feathers of the owl, and the horns of the buffalo, are parallel and specifically interchangeable developments?

Consider the vine, with its stem, branches, twigs, roots, rootlets, leaves, tendrils, and the luscious grapes of the ripe cluster. From one seed sprang all of these. On the bough of an orange tree there live and grow together leaf and petiole, flower and fruit, the green unripe fruit, the yellow and the golden-ripe. All these from one seed. Yet there is no jealousy among them. No one disowns a kindred origin for the root of the tree and its golden fruit, utterly unlike as these are, but, like so many other utterly unlike things in this world, sprung from the same germ.

To have produced and accumulated the vast divergences that now exist, a lapse of time, indeed, must be conceded, unmeasured and perhaps immeasurable; but this lapse of time is precisely what geology, independently of Darwinism, has already demanded. As the Scriptures speak of the earth as immoveable, because so it is in reference to the senses of man, they speak also of the everlasting mountains, and with them the rocks are a type of the eternal: compared with the life of man these expressions are truthful and well-chosen, but they do not mean to say the rocks are as eternal as God, nor yet everlasting compared with the existence of the globe. It may have taken ten thousand centuries to rear up a mountain, and yet, if we reckon the age of the globe on the scale of a man's life, the mountain be but of yesterday.

The immense antiquity, not only of the globe, but of that thin crust of it open to our inspection, has been ascertained by geology. Geology, again, has made it certain that during millions of years, changes on the earth's surface have been in continual progress, so that not once merely, but many times over, continents and oceans must have yielded to one another, yet by no sudden, but ever by a gradual transposition, such as is in constant progress at the present day.

Seeing that the dwelling-place of living creatures is thus continually and continuously changing, how clumsy an arrangement it would have been had the forms of life been made constant, instead of being endowed, as they clearly have been, with a wonderful power of adaptation. The question, be it remembered, is not for a moment whether God has made the universe, but *how* He has made that portion of it which He has enabled us to see and examine. Nor yet, to be thoroughly accurate, is it in question *how* He has worked, but how He has been pleased to exhibit His operations to the reasoning minds of men. What is worthy of God we cannot indeed judge. We can only believe that the things which are, stand worthiest of

His wisdom and goodness, whatever faults may seem in them to our rashly-judging short-sightedness. But comparing theories of creation according to human notions, is it a nobler conception that God should have made successively groups of beings to fill the world, and then swept them away to make room for others nearly like them; each time, as it were, improving on His first idea, and so arguing the imperfection of what had gone before by the very improvement of what followed; or that, foreseeing the perfect types from the beginning, He should have called into existence seeds of life capable, under the laws He gave them, of rising in successive generations through countless ages, to endowments of the noblest order, to a conscious life, to a reasoning faculty, to a moral sense, to a knowledge of God? In such an origin there is for man no degradation, since the lowliness of his parentage has ever been traced back to the dust of the ground; and the lowest form of life is higher in our imaginations than the dull brute earth. Indeed, if we desire to exalt our self-appreciation, whether is it grander for us to have been the work of an instant, or to have been elaborated with Divine care through millions of ages? Will not any miracle in our behalf, however stupendous, seem more credible on the latter than on the former supposition? When we see what Development has already done for the human species, we can the more readily imagine what, under the same Lawgiver, it may do in the future for the individuals of our race. When we find it possible or probable that our own bodies contain resemblances to ancestors enormously remote in time, simply because they contain atoms from the bodies of those very ancestors living again in ourselves, we can understand how in a future, whether near or enormously remote, atoms from the very body of the man that dies may be called into a renewed existence, and clothed again with all that is necessary to personal identity, though haply more transformed and higher raised above the old self, than would be an orang-outang or a naked savage, were either of these enabled to combine the chivalric courtesy of Sir Philip Sydney with the genius of Sophocles and Shakespeare.

THE NOACHIAN FLOOD[1].

DARWINISM implies almost throughout that no universal Deluge has drowned our globe, either within the last ten thousand years, or even within a period indefinitely longer. Let us speak with due respect of the contrary belief. It *seems* to rest upon the testimony of a Volume the most precious in the world. It was taken for granted till a few years back as much in science as in religion. For a while, the arguments that began to be raised against it were met by counter-arguments so plausible, and the objectors differed so widely among themselves, that unscientific opinion had a kind of right and prudence in adhering to that which had been taught for centuries, and was still taught without deviation in nursery, and school, and pulpit.

We should have asserted a better right and shown a higher prudence, had we waited, in a matter which concerned science full as much as it concerned religion,

[1] The design of this Essay was not, as has been erroneously supposed, to disprove the universality of the Deluge by help of Darwinism, but to remove one great obstacle to the general acceptance of Darwinism by disproving the universality of the Deluge. Taking the Theory of Development for granted, a recent universal Deluge would be too obviously impossible to need arguing against.

till, by learning facts and weighing arguments, we had become able to form an opinion no longer unscientific, or, at the very least, to appreciate the difficulties involved in the ancient belief.

We are forced to take a controversy of this kind as it stands; otherwise, there is a simple principle which ought to make all controversy on the subject needless. All authors endowed with common sense, let alone divine inspiration, use language which their intended readers may be expected to understand, and language appropriate to the scope and design of their writings. Unless, therefore, we suppose that the Old Testament writers proposed to teach natural science to the Hebrew nation, we ought to expect from them what we actually find: as to natural phenomena, past and present, they use the language not of far-advanced knowledge and minute particular research, but simply the language current in their own day and nation.

But, setting aside the general principle, in the present instance there is a second possibility of quashing the controversy, if it can be shown or made probable that the author, whose narrative is in question, never meant to imply that which for thousands of years has been held to be his meaning.

The whole point at issue is the *universality* of the Noachian Deluge, and the narrative has been thought to be uncompromising in its declarations that all the earth, to the very mountain-tops, was indeed enveloped in water, and, excepting the handful rescued in the ark, that all men and cattle and creeping things and fowls of the air were inexorably destroyed. But to this view of the narrative there is more than one objection upon the very surface of the narrative itself. And, by way of preface, let it be remarked how vague and indefinite is the use in ordinary language of such terms as 'all' and 'every' and 'universal.' For instance, if a popular lady gives a kettledrum, we say, 'all the world was at it,' although 500 persons could not have been squeezed into the rooms without being suffocated; or we say, ' so and so is a thing which every school-boy knows,' when we only mean that a good many lads of a particular age, in a particular rank of life, and belonging to one particular country, have most probably been taught it. And again we say, 'smoking is universal with the Dutch,' without implying that every baby in Holland has a pipe instead of a rattle. You are not to suppose that this is a view of language invented for the occasion, frivolously explaining grave and sacred composition by the trivialities of common speech. On the contrary, it is precisely to the unquestioned prevalence of such phraseology, in all but the most exact scientific writing, that the late Dr. M'Caul appealed, and appealed successfully, against more than one of the objections to the authority of the Pentateuch, which were raised some time ago by the well-known and ingenious arithmetician who presides over the see of Natal. When we read that 'there went out a decree from Cæsar Augustus that *all the world* should be taxed: and *all* went to be taxed, *every one* into his own city,' are we to infer either that the clever practical Roman decreed the taxation of barbarians over whom he had not the faintest shadow of control, or that every Israelite, without exception, found and visited his ancestral home in Palestine—merchants from Gades and Ophir and Tarshish, slaves and prisoners, sucking children, bed-ridden old men, dying sufferers? We shall not, if we are wise, shut up either Cæsar Augustus or the Evangelist St. Luke to so preposterous a meaning.

In this and ten thousand other instances, our general knowledge of the attendant circumstances, or what we call 'the nature of the case,' supplies the necessary exceptions. To have them all drawn out in detail would be tedious and troublesome. Suppose a glorious comet is about to make its appearance, and some astronomer publicly advises every one to be on the look-out for it on a certain night, how ridiculous would he appear if he made express exception of persons on the other side of the globe, of persons immured in dungeons, of persons not yet born, of persons who were blind, of persons who were dead! Yet an author, writing some three or four thousand years back, and borrowing perhaps from picture-records, certainly from the traditions, however delivered, of an age long anterior to his own, when language was far less ample and precise than it has since become, is treated as though every word must bear the full and exact force which it would have in a carefully-written treatise upon logic in the present day. We may assume that the author either had sound and accurate information in the ordinary course of human tradition, or else that he was endowed with a superhuman knowledge of the historical events in question.

But, on either assumption, what conceivable warrant have we for imagining that he was deprived of common sense? Either he knew the contradictions which natural science offers to the belief in a recent universal deluge, or he did not know them. If he knew them, we may infer from his silence that his narrative was not open to those contradictions; in other words, that the deluge of which he speaks was not universal. If he did not know them, his ignorance points to the same conclusion: otherwise, we shall have a divine miracle, intended for the warning and the benefit of the human race, yet so contrived that all its most surprising circumstances should be absolutely unknown to one half of mankind, and as absolutely incredible to the other half.

The historical account informs up that 'the waters prevailed exceedingly upon the earth; and all the high hills that were under the whole heaven were covered. Fifteen cubits upwards did the waters prevail; and the mountains were covered.' But Europe possesses mountains rising to a height of more than 10,000 cubits or 15,000 feet—one peak in Asia is 29,000 feet above the level of the sea—so that, on the common interpretation, the waters of the flood must have risen to a thickness above the ordinary sea-level of nearly 30,000 feet over the whole of the globe. But, on this supposition, the narrative is not only bewildering and morally impossible, but positively untruthful, for it declares the physical means employed in the production of the flood to be the fountains of the great deep and the rain from heaven— means entirely sufficient to produce a partial flood over a limited area, but utterly and ludicrously inadequate to produce a total deluge enveloping 'all the high hills under the whole heaven.' The notion is self-contradictory that the ocean can be employed to raise its own level, or that its general height can be increased by the rain which it is its own part to supply. Nor is there any indication afforded that a supernatural supply of water was added to our planet, to the extent of several hundred millions of cubic miles of liquid, which would have been required for the purpose of drowning the Caucasus and the Alps and Teneriffe and Popocatapetl and Chimilari. We must consider also the difficulty of breathing, and the intense cold that would have been experienced at that stupendous altitude. There is the old question of space in the ark; there is the old question of the food-supply, sufficient and appropriate, to be stored and sorted for its various occupants, carnivorous and herbivorous, beasts of prey, carrion-birds, and amphibious monsters. But what are these compared with the question how life could be sustained in the bitter freezing atmosphere, thousands of feet above the line of perpetual snow, by creatures accustomed to the lowlands of the tropics? Supposing, however, the atmosphere to have been completely warmed by the rise of the ocean, or even if the air within the ark was kept warm by its enormous crowd of denizens, we are confronted by a new difficulty, one that might seem laughable and improper to mention but for its vast and pressing importance in our own days, thwarting the physician, perplexing the statesman, baffling the chemist and the engineer. To this supposed epitome of the world's inhabitants, shut up for months within the ark, who were the scavengers?

But suppose every one of these problems to be solved by a miracle, although of such miracles not a hint is given, there still remains the statement to be dealt with, that 'God made a wind to pass over the earth, and the waters assuaged.' Surely this, if nothing else, is conclusive that the writer had all along been describing a local and partial deluge upon which a wind could have some sensible effect, not an universal flood wrapping all the mountains of the globe in water, in which case the mightiest wind that ever was, or could be dreamed of, could only have laid bare the surface of the land by piling up great hills and precipices of water upon the ocean.

When we wish to expose the miracles of a false religion or of a superstitious aberrant creed, we point out, as the case may be, that they are frivolous, useless, unmeaning, devoid of adequate motive, the end achieved and the means employed bearing no reasonable proportion; or we show that the testimony in their favour is inconsistent with itself, or that the consequences which should have flowed from the miracle, had it been genuine, are certainly wanting, unless, to bolster up one extreme improbability, a hundred others are invented and swallowed. To every one of these imputations the common theory of the Noachian Deluge lies open. But concede a few grains of common sense to the narrator; read his narrative in the spirit in which such a person must have written it; remember that he is not writing a scientific treatise, nor using the phraseology of modern Europe; bear in mind that he is speaking in an idiom no longer or now but seldom used, yet a just and noble idiom, which ascribes to God all that is done upon earth, whether good or evil, the works of man and the common processes of nature, as well as things superhuman and miraculous; and, with these considerations before us, we shall save the venerable record from every imputation, either of folly or of falsehood.

That which we have described to us is a vast penal catastrophe sweeping away some great centre of civilization by means of a terrible inundation. Along some ocean-border the far-stretching plains were dotted thickly with towns and villages. There were fields waving with corn; the vine and the olive, the orange and the palm abounded; there were cattle feeding in green pastures beside the still waters; there were populous tribes and nations carrying on all the business and revelry of life; they bought, they sold, they builded, they planted, they were marrying and giving in marriage, when suddenly the fountains of the great deep were broken up, and the earthquake wave rolled in upon them, and swept all the beauty and the glory and the sin remorselessly away. At the same time, the angry heavens were overcast, and the floodgates of the clouds poured down their volumes of ceaselessly-descending rain. The distant mountains were torn from the sight; nay, every high hill under the whole heaven was itself covered and enfolded in a liquid veil, for every rill was now a torrent, every tiny silver thread of a cascade now a dark unbroken avalanche of waters. One family alone, alone obedient to the warning which all had received, were saved amidst this universal ruin, and took with them into the ark of their refuge specimens of every bird and beast and creeping thing that their own country produced, and that was in any way serviceable to man. When cloud and mist had rolled away from the mountain-tops, when the face of the ground was once more dry—with these creatures they stocked their new settlement. The well-watered plain was speedily replenished; the vine flourished; the cattle brought forth abundantly; the children of the patriarch multiplied rapidly and spread far and wide over their rich and undisputed inheritance.

Such is the narrative as it glimmers through the haze of forty centuries, only told in the original with unrivalled simplicity and force, grander than any description by forbearing to describe, told as one would tell it, who in that convulsion of nature had lost kindred, friends and countrymen, as one who had seen the whole world, so far as he knew it or cared for it, foundering in the waves, and yet had lived on through all the unutterable calamity to see himself once more surrounded by fruitful fields and smiling homesteads, and all that might make what was to him emphatically a new world the counterpart of the old.

Some may permit themselves for a moment to set aside the limitation we have suggested to the number of animals in the ark as fanciful and unwarranted. It will be proper therefore to draw out the consequences attaching to the old opinion. We find from the words of the narrative, that the patriarch Noah was intrusted with the task of collection. To achieve it, then, he must have gone in person, or sent expeditions, to Australia for the kangaroo and the wombat, to the frozen North for the Polar bear, to Africa for the gorilla and the chimpanzee; the hippopotamus of the Nile, the elk, the bison, the dodo, the apteryx, the emeu and the cassowary must have been brought together by vast efforts from distant quarters. The patriarch or his agents must have been endowed with a supernatural knowledge of natural history far surpassing Solomon's or that of our own times, that they might properly distinguish varieties and species, so that no species might be omitted and none represented by more than one variety. To accomplish this with the minutest insects, they must have been provided with powerful microscopes. Every portion of the dry land of the globe must have been accessible to them; every jungle, cavern, and ravine. The little islands that lose themselves in mid-ocean must all have been ransacked; the search, too, that might not neglect any acre of ground in all the continents of the world, would be distracted with the most varied and incongruous pursuits. Sheep, game, caterpillars, beasts of prey, snails, eagles, fleas and titmice, must all have their share of attention. Unusual pains must be employed to secure them uninjured. They must be fed and cared for during a journey, perhaps, of thousands of miles, till they reach the ark; they must be hindered from devouring one another while the search is continued for rats and bats and vipers and toads and scorpions, and other animals which a patriarch, specially singled out as just and upright and a lover of peace, would naturally wish and naturally be selected to transmit as a boon to his favoured descendants.

It might be asked how, with the supernatural knowledge requisite for collecting all the terrestrial animals of the globe, and the unique opportunity for observation afforded by a residence of some months with them in the ark, no more scientific classification was arrived at than that into birds and beasts and creeping things? But letting this pass, or scattering it and other objections to the winds by inventing a miracle to explain the gathering together of the animals, we shall then have to give some account of their re-distribution. Instead of worrying ourselves with the problem, shall we at once solve it by asserting that they were miraculously re-transferred to the habitations from which they came? This will be a highly satisfactory plan, if only it will stop the mouths of those inquisitive persons who never know when they are beaten in an argument. But one cavil may easily be foreseen, requiring a new miracle to satisfy it; for many of the animals must either have been miraculously supplied with provisions, or miraculously enabled to do without them; or else, to take a single instance, two spiders would have been limited to a couple of flies, and when the flies had become extinct, because devoured by the spiders, the spiders also would have become extinct through having no more flies to devour; and thus their preservation in the ark, at the expense of a great many unrecorded and highly improbable miracles, would have been utterly useless.

Suppose, however, that they were spread over the earth again by the slow process of natural distribution. Certain perplexities, indeed, may have arisen when they first issued from the ark, when the cobra and the rattlesnake, the hungry wolf and the relentless tiger were let loose upon the impoverished world and its defenceless inhabitants. For at that conjuncture to have destroyed even one cruel and venomous beast might have blotted out a whole species. It is surely a little remarkable that ravenous beasts and birds of prey should have been limited, even while in the ark, to feeding upon animals in a ceremonial or ecclesiastical sense clean; but if, after they had left the ark, and had once more to provide for themselves, the wily panther and the treacherous hyena must be imagined debating before every meal whether their victim belonged to the sevens of the clean or the couples of the unclean animals, shall we not turn in pity and vexation from any view that involves and admits so monstrous a supposition?

But we will concede that every creature bore a charmed life, that it might not perish by famine or violence till it had propagated its kind. We should then expect to observe that species had distributed themselves over the globe in lines either tortuous or direct, single or branching, broad or narrow, but all diverging from a common centre. Yet nothing of the kind is found. On the contrary, the species of the new world differ from those of the old, the species of one continent from those of another[1]. The marsupials of Australia and Polynesia are generically distinct from all other animals on the globe except the opossum. The elephant of Africa is not the same species as the elephant of India : so with the lion, so with the rhinoceros. The apes and baboons of the old world are nowhere to be found in America, nor the American monkeys anywhere in the old world. In Madagascar, separated from Africa by less than the breadth of England, all the species except one, and nearly all the genera, are peculiar[2]. Everywhere species are found limited in their range by natural barriers, such as climate, rivers, mountains, oceans. Are we to suppose that the prisoners could scramble into their prisons, and then suddenly became incapable of scrambling out again ? Everywhere, as a rule, this range is consistent with the hypothesis of an origin central to the range, inconsistent with that of an origin distant from it. Where, as on mountain ranges, we find, contrary to the general rule, the same species in different localities, the migration from the door of the ark loses all semblance of probability, unless we are pleased to imagine that creatures, now without the instinct of migration, for a long time possessed it, and roamed about the world through many a sultry plain to pick out a hill-side here and there with a temperature suited to their constitutions. But the exceptional phenomenon, otherwise so hard to account for, Darwin has admirably explained, by pointing out that species adapted

---

[1] Lyell, 'Principles of Geology,' ii. 332.   [2] Ibid. ii. 344.

to a low temperature would naturally have occupied lowlands in the Glacial Period, from which, as the cold gradually grew less and less intense, they would as naturally have retired, some of them northwards, others to the cool heights of various mountains.

That there was a Glacial Period, when great icebergs travelled over England, a period geologically as but of yesterday, though enormously more remote than any historical dates, is now beyond all question. Equally beyond question is it that countless ages and generations of living beings on the earth preceded that Glacial Period. And, added to this, we find that there are forms of life just where they would have been left by the effect of that period, had there been an unbroken succession from that time to this, and just where it is most unlikely they should be found, had they been forced to travel to those habitations from the door of the ark within the practically insignificant period of 4300 years.

But still further, we may compare the world of life before the Flood with the world of life since. And here surely it needs not the genius of Darwin or Lyell or Owen to perceive the conclusiveness of the argument which their genius has pointed out and enforced. For instance, where the marsupials now live, there lived marsupials in ages long before Noah, as the fossil remains testify. The fossils are fossil marsupials, but marsupials of species now extinct. So that the 'door of the ark' theory requires us to believe that the marsupials found their way to Australia, leaving no traces of their route on land, crossing seas which they never subsequently recrossed, and planting themselves precisely in that region which other marsupials, generically the same but specifically different, had occupied before them.

We are to believe this of countless other species in all parts of the world. We are to believe that they slowly and in many generations worked their way back to these quasi-ancestral homes, and yet neglected to occupy vast tracts equally or even better adapted to their wants. We must believe also that some of the fleetest, strongest, and most sagacious animals, as the horse and the elephant, failed to trace out the abodes of their ancient representatives, since America, when discovered a few years ago, possessed these quadrupeds only in fossil and in no living species [1].

There is indeed one animal, whose powers of contrivance would account for its distribution over the globe, even supposing it to have begun with a single family, not more than 4300 years ago, and to have ranged from a single centre. Man is that animal. Yet, if all the other facts that bear on the universality of the Noachian Deluge were in an agreement with it as entire as their irreconcileability is utter and complete, still the circumstances of the human race alone would disable us from believing that the Flood of Noah's epoch extended over all the globe. With other animals it might be advanced that the different species and main varieties had been represented in the ark and were thence disseminated; but in the case of man we are precluded from such an explanatory device by the express terms

[1] Lyell, ii. 336.

of the diluvian record. If the Noachian Flood was universal, then from Noah alone must be descended all the races of man now upon the earth: all the great and curious variations they display must have been evolved, not in countless generations as Darwinism supposes, but in some two or three hundred or less. From Noah alone must have sprung within a mere handful of centuries races so widely unlike one another as Greeks and Negroes, Jews and Egyptians, Saxons and Ojibbeways, Caffirs and Hottentots, Fuegians and Patagonians, Californians and Chinese, Arabs and Esquimaux. In the same archipelago we have the Malay, the Papuan, and the dwarf snub-nosed Negrito. To give the contrast between the two former in the words of Mr. Wallace[1]:—
'The Malay is of short stature, brown-skinned, straight-haired, beardless, and smooth-bodied. The Papuan is taller, is black-skinned, frizzly-haired, bearded, and hairy-bodied. The former is broad-faced, has a small nose, and flat eyebrows; the latter is long-faced, has a large and prominent nose, and projecting eyebrows. The Malay is bashful, cold, undemonstrative, and quiet; the Papuan is bold, impetuous, excitable, and noisy. The former is grave, and seldom laughs; the latter is joyous and laughter-loving,—the one conceals his emotions, the other displays them.' Such is the description and contrast of two types of mankind geographically separated from one another by an interval of not more than 300 miles; yet the line which separates these two races of the human family is almost exactly coincident with that

---

[1] 'The Malay Archipelago,' vol. ii. p. 448.

deep-sea line which forms the boundary between two great zoological provinces. Either, then, in these two distinct but neighbouring localities, the whole multitude of species, man included, must have been undergoing variation simultaneously for tens of thousands of years, or else the differences in the whole multitude, man included, must have been already established, or nearly so, when first they stepped forth in singular procession from the door of the ark. But the former alternative, which is the Darwinian, is consistent with the record of the Noachian Flood in implying that the inundation was only partial; while the latter alternative contradicts the record in an essential point on which it is perfectly explicit, by necessitating the presence in the ark of more than one human family.

As long as we are content to speak of 4000 years or so, some one might be tempted to fancy, however erroneously, that such a period would be adequate to produce the existing varieties of mankind, because there is some evidence of comparatively rapid changes of colour having taken place under the influence of climate, and because a new type of features appears to be forming itself with a noticeable progress under the absolutely unique circumstances which have governed the recent colonization of North America. Unique those circumstances are, because never before has there been so much mingling of the blood of different nations and races in a new and unoccupied field, with much to stimulate and nothing to curb or repress variation. Never before have men's minds and bodies in every faculty been so taxed and strained to activity by the very superabundance of their resources, the virgin soil of a new country, an inherited civilization, enormous and ever-enlarging facilities for doing, for living, moving, and learning—facilities sometimes that cannot be declined or escaped from, though they 'fret the pigmy body to decay, and o'er-inform the tenement of clay.'

But, in truth, there is no question of 4000 years in the matter; for there were black people in the time of Herodotus and in the time of Solomon. Already in the time of Moses there existed a race in Palestine so different from the Israelites, that the first Hebrew explorers were daunted by the sight of them, although, in fact, they were looking on a race no longer in its prime, but one that was dying out. Egyptian monuments, dating back to the same period and earlier, give representations of Africans, Asiatics, and Europeans, with their physical characteristics then as now unmistakeably distinct; they portray the Negro as the Negro still is both in colour and in features[1].

If it took only 800 years, then, which is the interval between the Flood and the birth of Moses, to originate and establish types so distinct as Jews, Egyptians, Negroes, and Anakim, all gathered together in a little corner of the world, might not Nature, having done so much in so short a time for the highest animal, do a little more in a longer time for lower animals, and so supply that origin of species by variation for which

---

[1] 'Genesis of the Earth and of Man,' p. 117; quoted in Sir J. Lubbock's 'Prehistoric Times,' p. 314.

Mr. Darwin contends? Would not the obvious inference be that Nature had done so, if it were not fancied that such an origin of species was still more repugnant to the Book of Genesis than even a limitation of the area covered by the Flood? But the Darwinian theory, happily for itself, is not dependent upon any supposition so incredible as one which would warrant us in expecting among the descendants, for example, of William the Conqueror, people as little like one another as John Bull and John Chinaman, Uncle Sambo and the last of the Mohicans. There are circumstances of immense weight to convince us that certain marked divisions of mankind originated in the regions which they are now occupying. There are other circumstances preponderating for the common origin of mankind. Darwinism has at length shown how these phenomena can be reconciled, by simply connecting the history of man with that vast duration of life upon the globe which geological science has unveiled. The likenesses among races of men demand a common parentage for all those races; the unlikenesses can only be accounted for on the view of an isolation immensely protracted of one race from another. Thus the primary origin is common to all; the secondary origin is peculiar to each: but now that the primary origin has been proved to be so vastly more remote than was once supposed, the secondary origin recedes of itself into a far distant past, to give time for differences to arise and develope, since, if the actually existing unlikenesses were only skin-deep, instead of affecting, as they do, the bones of the skeleton and the whole fibre of the mind, they would still be too great to admit a common derivation of the whole human family from the patriarch Noah.

What Geology teaches to demonstration is, that all parts of the dry land have been not once only but many times under the waters of the ocean; but it teaches likewise to demonstration that at least for many and many an age, almost beyond our powers of conceiving duration of time, there has been no total submergence of the land. That interchange of lake and sea with isle and continent which is now going on under our eyes, has been going on for ages innumerable. By this and kindred means human beings, like all kinds of animals and all kinds of plants, have at intervals experienced severance into groups and isolation. Thus has mankind been broken up into distinct families, at first with no line of demarcation except the geographical, but gradually in successive generations becoming more and more unlike in manners, morals, language, features, intelligence, and civilization. But since the era of the Noachian Deluge neither has there been time for Nature, with her slow though certain processes, to effect so great a reconstruction of barriers as to break up the human family, if till then continuous and united; nor, if there had been time for the geographical severance, would there have been time for the constitutional changes.

Among the ancients some believed that the sun, moon, and stars were in reality about the size which they appear to the unassisted eyesight; others supposed the vault of the sky to be a revolving dome of solid crystal pierced with little holes through which men saw in starry shapes the fire of the ethereal region beyond it. Persons with such ideas of space and physical science might not readily have accepted on the moment the Copernican system of astronomy. In the same way persons with a narrow and limited view of the duration of time may find a difficulty in receiving arguments based on or implying the enormous extent of it, which all sciences are now combining to demonstrate. But this mental incapacity, the result of false education and early prejudice, may be defied to resist any real investigation of the facts or study of what has been written upon them. Let any man of mature mind and average intellect read through Sir John Lubbock's 'Prehistoric Times,' Mr. Darwin's 'Origin of Species,' and Sir Charles Lyell's 'Principles of Geology,' and retain if he can the opinion that our globe was first peopled about 6000 years ago, and subsequently all but depopulated by an universal Flood. Let him see, indeed, whether he can read Sir Charles Lyell's account of the progress of opinion and controversy on these subjects and refrain from blushing. He will recognize in that account a turmoil and clamour of fools and philosophers, of laymen and divines. He will have to set to the credit of intelligent humanity and enlightened Christendom a long tissue of pious frauds, jesuitical defences, arguments based on imaginary facts, and facts perverted by imagination, till he comes down to the present time and finds a great multitude of all classes at length agreed in affirming that life has endured on the globe with unbroken continuity through a past as yet unfathomable. His own mind, he will perceive, has actually reached maturity without having admitted the voice of this multitude, although, to apply almost literally the words of his great Master, 'If these should hold their peace, the stones would cry out[1].'

The world and its wonders are of no mushroom growth, although even the mushroom, which is commonly supposed to spring up in a single night, requires a much longer period, often many weeks, for its production[2]. The Book of Genesis itself most clearly warns any careful reader against attempting to build a chronology upon the brief memoranda of names and dates which for other reasons are inserted in it. For, taking them simply as they stand, Shem, the son of Noah, is represented as long surviving the birth of Isaac, while Abraham, the father of Isaac, appears as the contemporary of a vast number of different and strange tribes and nations— Egyptians, Philistines, Canaanites, Syrians, and many more, besides the Chaldeans from among whom he came. To find a parallel to all this, we should imagine our own Edward III, instead of dying in 1377 as he did, living on and on to the present day, a forgotten old man, not noticed in the page of history throughout 500 eventful years, during which the whole of Europe was becoming peopled with descendants of himself and his

---

[1] A religious and supremely orthodox poet of the last century enquires, 'Where is the dust that has not been alive?'—Young, 'Night Thoughts,' Night IX, l. 87.

[2] 'Mushrooms and Toadstools.'—Worthington G. Smith, p. 17.

father, men speaking languages mutually unintelligible, holding creeds mutually abhorrent, with strange diversities in dress, manners and government, and some prevented by national custom from even eating at the same table with guests of another neighbouring and kindred tribe. In vain should we search through history for any actual parallel, for any instance of developments so extraordinary, and estrangements so complete, occurring within a space of only 500 years. If all the nations spoken of as contemporary with Abraham were only 500 years distant from the Flood, as the Book of Genesis shows them to have been, we may be certain that they could trace back their lineage, independently of Noah and his family, far beyond the era of the Deluge. The monumental evidence of Egyptian chronology carries us back to a Pharaoh reigning some three or four hundred years before that date[1]. The Book of Genesis introduces us to another Pharaoh reigning some 400 years after it. Are we to set aside the monumental evidence, and make this later Pharaoh a descendant of Noah, reigning as a powerful monarch, while Abraham, the rightful heir of a patriarchal monarchy over all the earth, was nothing but a wandering shepherd? Religion, morals, civilization, as far as we know anything about them in those ages, whether we regard their advancement in some quarters or their decay in others, all protest against having their progress cramped into those four or five hundred years. They protest against being ascribed with all their conspicuous diversities to the offspring of

[1] 'Genesis of the Earth and of Man,' pp. 113, 114.

one man, whose son, grandson, great-grandson and great-great-grandson, Shem, Arphaxad, Salah, and Eber, were actually still living during all these supposed revolutions[1].

Indeed, if we go back from our 400 to our 4000 years, the protests on these points are almost equally forcible. In the matter of language, estimate how many generations must have passed away before the children of a common parent came to vary in speech as much as Chinese, Russians, Englishmen, and clucking Hottentots. Form some estimate of the time required for the rise and growth of civilization, not only in the old-world centres of Nineveh and Babylon and Egyptian Thebes, but in the separate and independent centres of Mexico and Peru. Explain, moreover, what, on the hypothesis of a common Noachian descent, must be called the rise and growth of barbarism. Show, if it be possible, how, amidst the rapid strides of civilization, side by side with the advancement of taste, literature, and science, the descendants of Noah in some cases degenerated from all culture, sank away from all morality, lost all religion, forgot all useful arts, even those most essential to the lowest degree of comfort, the kindling of fire, the use of metals, the construction of dwellings, while they learned the habits and acquired something more than the innocent shamelessness of brutes—learned to prefer the flesh of their own species to any other, learned to make a duty in some regions of putting their parents to death,

---

[1] Genesis, chap. xi.

in others, of eating their dead bodies[1]. Such customs we have on record four centuries before Christ, such customs on record as existing nineteen centuries after. Will any one attempt to persuade us that the savages of Andaman and the Feejee Islands are cousins, through an ancestor no more remote than Noah, of Chatham and Wilberforce, and Lesseps and Brunel?

Traditions of a Deluge, it is true, are found almost everywhere. The reason doubtless is that almost everywhere some tremendous calamity of this description has at one time or another occurred. Inundations on a small scale are common and frequent, but on a scale great enough to surprise the imagination and become traditional in the memories of a people, they would naturally be rare and infrequent in the extreme, so that the fact of such an experience belonging to the history of so many different races, is but another proof, or at least another indication, of the antiquity of man. If stress is to be laid on the points of similarity between the traditions, as proving that every land has been ravaged by the waters of a flood, equal stress may in fairness be laid on the points of difference, as proving that not one common universal Deluge is spoken of, but many separate and partial floods, distinct in time, in place, and in results. If stress again is to be laid on the tradition because it is common to so many tribes, let equal importance be granted to the traditions of time among the Chaldeans and the Egyptians, the Chinese and the Hindus, who

---

[1] Sir John Lubbock, 'Prehistoric Times,' pp. 338, 346, 452; Herodotus, iv. 26.

reckon the years of their uninterrupted histories by tens of thousands [1].

Finally, we may ask, where are the traces of so tremendous and unparalleled a convulsion as one that could wrap the whole world in water, and hold all its dædal beauty for many months in that drowned condition, till a tempest still more furious and unparalleled drave heaven and earth, the clouds and ocean, once more asunder? We know how the little trilobite in the Devonian seas behaved in its hour of peril millions of years back; we know what food men ate long ages before the Flood, what weapons they used, what houses they built, what animals they tamed; but what became of man and beast and bird and forest in the supposed universal Deluge, no one knows. The signs and natural monuments of the catastrophe, which should have been visible or discoverable on every side, can nowhere be ascertained,—things that the waters should have swept away or torn down they have left undisturbed, shell-mounds and glacier moraines and boulderstones on the mountain-side; while the great museum of the dead which they should have formed, one would think, over all the earth, to constitute one striking and indisputable geological date, as well as a world-wide monument of religion, is nowhere to be found.

What became of flower and herb, of creatures that live between the zones of high and low water, of mollusk and coral and fish that require an appropriate depth and a fitting temperature in their liquid homes, it will be

[1] See Mill's 'History of British India,' book ii. ch. i. and notes.

useless to speculate, if, after all that has been urged upon other points, there are some who still think that the description in Genesis is the description of a Flood that prevailed over all the world, and intend still to believe in such a Flood, and to teach it as a part of religious doctrine, notwithstanding any argument or scientific proof to the contrary. For them we can do no more than commend to their daily reflection a few lines from the lives of two famous men:—' In spite,' says Dr. Wilson, ' alike of the science and the devout religious spirit of Columbus, the Salamanca divines pronounced the idea of the earth's spherical form heterodox, and a belief in antipodes incompatible with the historical traditions of our faith: since to assert that there were inhabited lands on the opposite side of the globe would be to maintain that there were nations not descended from Adam, it being impossible for them to have passed the intervening ocean. This would therefore be to discredit the Bible, which expressly declares that all men are descended from one common parent[1].' And thus another author describes a well-known incident in the life of Galileo:—' Clad in a penitent's sackcloth, the mighty, self-relying philosopher and genius fell upon his knees, and, with his hands laid on the Holy Evangelists, declared that he abjured, detested, and would never again teach, the doctrine of the sun's stability and the earth's motion. Having confirmed his oath in writing, and promised to perform the enjoined penance, he rose from his knees a pardoned man; and turning about

[1] ' Prehistoric Man,' Dr. Daniel Wilson, p. 101.

to one of his friends, stamped on the ground, and pronounced in an emphatic whisper, " Eppure si muove [1]," —but still it *does* move.'

As the antipodes exist, as the earth goes round the sun, and as the Bible continues to be true, in spite of the theologians and inquisitors at Salamanca and at Rome, so will it continue to be true and full of truth, when at length it shall be acknowledged, as it will be, that there is nothing universal about the Noachian Deluge except the disbelief in its universality.

[1] 'The Daughter of Galileo,' by the author of 'Mary Powell,' p. 283.

INSTINCT AND REASON.

An initial probability has been established by Mr. Darwin and Mr. Wallace that the reason or mind of man, as well as his body, has attained its present complete excellence through gradual development. No one denies that, between a man's birth and his prime of life, time is required for the intellectual powers to unfold; but it demands an effort which few have as yet made to see in this progression of the individual mind a compendious history of the indefinitely slow process by which the human mind itself has been formed, passing upward, step by step, from simple vitality, dawning consciousness, the various grades of so-called instinct, to the full capacities of the most enlightened reason.

The theory of development or evolution has excited immense opposition and distrust, because of its obvious application to the human body. Its application to the human mind, which, though less obvious at the first glance, almost inevitably follows, seems to have inspired Mr. Wallace himself with alarm. He winds up the admirable series of essays in which he supports the theory under discussion with one that earnestly propounds 'the *limits* of natural selection as applied to man.' His arguments on this subject are drawn from physical science, though his mind is evidently, and even confessedly, swayed throughout by other than physical considerations. He represents, in fact, and endeavours to reconcile to his own scientific views, the weight of popular prejudice which has hitherto condemned those views with some vehemence of opposition.

The sentiment in question amounts to this, that certain powers or faculties of the human mind are so wonderful and so unique, that they could not have originated in the ordinary processes of nature without some special intervention. Antecedents conforming to the usual observed order in other living productions are not sufficiently magnificent for the soul of man. Something sudden, something mysterious, is demanded in the agency of its creation. It must be like Pallas Athene, springing from the brain of Zeus, a goddess fully armed from her birth in the panoply of wisdom and virtue. Yet the whole feeling thus to be described of what is fit and worthy must be accredited, as we desire to show, simply to prejudice. Nothing can really depend for its intrinsic grandeur upon our knowledge or ignorance of its origin. A single cause instantaneously producing its effect does not make the result in any way more admirable or magnificent than the like result coming at the close of an indefinitely extended chain of causation. Feelings of surprise and wonder are excited when we find that ten thousand copies of the *Times* newspaper can be printed within a single hour; but the same feelings move us in the granite-yards of Scotland, when we learn that many months are required for cutting through a single block. At the first proposal of railways, a pace of twenty or five-and-twenty miles an hour was thought too wonderful for belief; while now, from familiarity with far higher rates of speed, we think it miserably slow. A child is surprised to learn that the light of the sun requires time to reach the eye; but a new and even greater surprise is aroused by the information that the time so required is only a few minutes for ninety millions of miles. The swiftness of thought is proverbial. A single act of thought is commonly supposed to be absolutely instantaneous; and yet presence of mind, which depends on rapidity of thought, is fully recognized as an uncommon quality, while it has now been ascertained by experiment that every thought requires a definite, and in many cases measurable, length of time for its production and exercise. Following the analogy of these illustrations, we may expect that the popular opinion or prejudice as to the instantaneous creation of the human mind will vanish and subside when men become familiar with the idea of its slow development. It will at least be seen that there is no special dignity and grandeur in the supposed suddenness of its introduction into the universe. The general scheme of nature, so far as we can penetrate its working, seems to show that there is some proportion observed between the time spent in producing and the perfection of the thing produced. Religion itself is an unquestionable witness to this method of procedure. There is no great religion of which the adherents claim to have had it revealed to them from the first in its full perfection.

What is true of religion, is true of all arts and sciences. Their progress has been gradual. The greatness of nations, even when it seems to blaze forth in history most suddenly, ever finds its true origin in numerous steps of slow preparation. A hardy, frugal tribe of warriors is nursed in some obscure mountain cradle. The struggle for existence fosters their preservative virtues. A line of rulers is evoked, forced by the circumstances of their tenure to acquire, as their leading qualities, cunning, prudence, self-control, fertility of resource, promptitude of action, till at length the hour and the man coincide, and a handful of barbarians give their name to a great empire. The same rule prevails with languages, and the literatures that adorn them. So fully is this established in regard to literature, that men who examine the subject deeply are almost led to disbelieve in originality of genius altogether, from the invariable indebtedness of the noblest authors to the thoughts and imaginings of earlier minds. There is, therefore, no antecedent improbability that can fairly be pleaded against the gradual development of the human mind. On the contrary, every possible analogy is in its favour. A supposition so favoured becomes at least a lawful and reasonable subject of enquiry. If it be true that the theory of evolution applies to the mind of man, we should expect to find in that mind itself traces of the earlier steps, or grades of development, through which it has passed, and also in the world around creatures lower than humanity in some sort representing those earlier stages of slowly unfolding reason. In other words, we should expect to find in human nature itself those very inequalities, that very conflict of the higher and the lower elements on which moralists so urgently insist, and we should expect to find affinities and resemblances, more or less close, pervading the whole animal creation, and exhibiting human reason and brute intelligence as, upon a broad view, one in kind, however different in degree.

The first requisite for intelligence is the possession of memory. Without this faculty, intelligence is impossible; but, on the other hand, memory that does not subserve some sort of intelligence, is a useless faculty; and in this the old theory of creation agrees with the new, that nothing obtains a footing in the world without a use. It may be urged, that the human memory is incomparably superior to that of the lower animals; but there are surprising differences in the powers of memory among human beings, and the effects of cultivation, with the facilities for that cultivation supplied by language, should be taken into account. It is important to observe also, that with brutes, as with men, some individuals are quicker than others; that the memory of brutes, like our own, can be improved by training; and that its powers are not equally distributed to all classes. The dog, the horse, the parrot, the elephant, are probably not further below mankind in the faculty of memory, than they are superior in it to the oyster and the jelly-fish.

To make the most of humanity, without introducing the question of man's material form and structure, one would naturally insist upon his docility or power of being taught; upon his versatility or power of adapting various means to the same or various ends; upon his moral nature, embracing the different passions and affections, and the knowledge of good and evil; and, lastly, no doubt, one would be inclined and one would have a right to insist on the grandeur of his aspirations. A crafty rhetorician would perhaps dwell on the collective value of these endowments, and then exhibit them, separately, rising to their height and fulness in men like Archimedes, and Chrysostom, and Dante. He would dare us to trace back the mental ancestry of these true heroes to apes and fishes. Yet the reason, piety, and imagination of such men, are themselves developed between childhood and maturity; their very pre-eminence shows that improvement in such qualities is possible from one generation to another, and that therefore meanness of origin needs only to be coupled with remoteness in time to reconcile the supremacy of man's intelligence with its ultimate derivation from the lowest powers of consciousness.

Mr. Wallace has pointed out very clearly and conclusively the fallacious character of the evidence on which the old theory of instinct was founded. Starting with the notion that wild animals had none of that docility and versatility which man possesses through his reasoning powers, yet seeing them produce effects like those which man produces by the help of teachers or his own choice of means, we inferred the existence of as many separate faculties as there are kinds of animals. Each of these faculties was thought to resemble reason about as much as a jack-in-the-box resembles a man. The faculty came into exercise in one invariable way without any choice on its owner's part, just as the jack starts up, whether he will or no, when his lid is taken off. We wondered at the admirable contrivance and design by which these very limited faculties were adapted in each case to the wants and preservation of the species to which they belonged. At times, it is true, with some inconsistency, we permitted ourselves to upbraid the goose with its stupidity; to speak of the sheep as silly, and the ostrich as wanting intelligence; we even expunged the dodo, with its self-preserving instinct, from the face of the earth; but in spite of these slips and mischances, we still kept gaping and wondering at our own explanation of things, and calling it an excessively wise and ingenious contrivance that every species of animal should have a separate faculty to itself, when one and the same faculty for them all would not only do just as well, but a great deal better. We were far from perceiving how strong a support to Materialism our theory involved, since if the lower animals without reason produce effects like those of reason, then effects like those of reason in a number of cases beyond calculation must be the result of bodily structure. It might not follow that the effects of reason itself were the results of bodily structure, but it would become startlingly probable.

 The history of domesticated animals is a continuous proof that some at least of the lower creatures are capable of learning, and how learning can be achieved without intelligence has never yet been explained, and is never likely to be. But Mr. Wallace points out that we have made a gratuitous assumption, unsupported by evidence, in supposing birds, for example, to build their nests by instinct rather than by following the example and instruction of their parents. Many things, he remarks, which we ourselves are said to do instinctively, such as putting out our hands to save ourselves from falling, are acquired habits, not instinctive actions, and in fact not possessed by infants. Mr. Darwin [1] tells us of a species of ant which behaves differently towards its slaves in England and in Switzerland respectively. In his memorable account of the busy bee, he shows that some species of bees are less clever at their work than others, and that the accuracy even of the most advanced cell-makers has been overrated. This is the more worthy to be noted, because the same persons who are extremely zealous to set forth reason as superior in kind to what they call instinct, are yet often eager to extol the effects of the lower faculty above those of the higher. An interesting account has recently been given of baboons in the neighbourhood of the Cape of Good Hope combining to pursue, and after a chase of two days and a night, successfully destroying a leopard which had invaded their haunts. Two tribes of baboons in the same locality, the occupants of separate rocky strongholds, are described as upon one occasion meeting in battle, the result being, that nearly a hundred

---

[1] 'Origin of Species,' p. 268.

were afterwards found dead or dying on the scene of action[1]. The shape of the creature, and the combination for warlike purposes, which carries with it such a tinge of humanity, can scarcely fail to affect the imagination. Yet these isolated instances must be far less telling than the comparison which Mr. Wallace has so ingeniously instituted between man as a builder and birds in the same capacity. The shelter of the savage is in many cases a less finished contrivance than the nest which the bird prepares for its young. The featherless biped, like the feathered one, takes the materials readiest to its digits. Generations upon generations follow one another without improvement or signs of inventive skill. Even in the days of enlightenment, and in nations which pride themselves most upon it, the human nest is repeatedly constructed without the smallest attention to comfort, health, or beauty. Men, whose fathers before them have built long rows of red-brick boxes to live in, build, by instinct if you will, for it can scarcely be by reason, more lengthening chains of red-brick boxes. There is no reason, indeed, for supposing that the bird consults any principle of beauty in the construction of its nest, but a principle of expedience some birds certainly do consult; the orchard oriole, for example, building its nest shallow or deep, according as it is placed among firm and stiff branches, or suspended from the slender wind-swayed twigs of the weeping-willow[2]. The fact that birds build in

[1] 'Good Words for the Young,' June 1870. Animal Defences. By A. W. Drayson.
[2] Wallace, 'Essays on Natural Selection,' p. 227.

human habitations, and make use of human manufactures, is a proof that they are capable of choice both as to locality and materials. The often-observed circumstance, that animals in a newly-discovered country are without fear of man,—a fear which they speedily acquire from experience of his mischievous propensities,—is a clear proof that they are capable of learning caution. It cannot be pretended that a caution which thus only comes in conjunction with experience is instinctive, or anything else than the result of observation, and therefore a sign of intelligent judgment. The lower animals, then, can learn prudence; can profit by experience. In the training of domesticated animals, the same motives of pleasure and pain are applied, and applied effectually, as are used in the education of human beings by parents and schoolmasters and lawgivers. This could not be if the groundwork of the moral nature were not the same in man and the lower animals. Addison was inclined to hold the old opinion, that 'God himself is the soul of brutes,' *Deus est anima brutorum*. 'One would wonder,' he says, 'to hear sceptical men disputing for the reason of animals, and telling us it is only our pride and prejudices that will not allow them the use of that faculty [1].' And yet his charming essays upon the natural history of animals, in which he took so keen a personal pleasure, with very little alteration, might be read as arguments in defence of the opinion he thus condemns. He remarks that birds, which ordinarily drive away their young as soon as they are able to get their own liveli-

---

[1] 'The Spectator,' No. 120.

hood, nevertheless continue to feed them if they are tied to the nest, or confined within a cage, or by any other means appear to be out of a condition of supplying their own necessities. He observes, that the brood-hen will leave her eggs longer in summer than in winter, because in summer they will cool less speedily. But apart from the ingenuity necessary for the propagation of the species, he considers the same bird to be a very idiot, without the least glimmering of thought or common sense, mistaking a piece of chalk for an egg, and sitting upon it as though it were one, insensible of an increase or diminution in the number of those she lays, not distinguishing between her own and those of another species; and when the birth appears of never so different a bird, cherishing it for her own.

It is curious that we should abuse the hen for being now and then deceived by our impostures, considering the immense quantities of counterfeit coin we ourselves accept as currency, and the strange compounds of chalk and mud and alum and poisonous herbs and minerals which, according to the analysts, we contentedly swallow down as milk and butter, bread and beer. But the hen in a wild state is not subject to our impositions, and possibly the domestic hen finds it better for herself to overlook them. At any rate, as the mistakes concern her progeny, if her conduct is other than beneficial, it is an argument *against* the perfection of instinct, which it tends to bring down to the level of imperfect human reason. It is commonly supposed that ducklings take to the water by instinct. And Addison tells us that on one occasion, as he was walking in the yard of his friend's country-house, he 'was wonderfully pleased to see the different workings of instinct in a hen followed by a brood of ducks. The young, upon the sight of a pond, immediately ran into it; while the step-mother, with all imaginable anxiety, hovered about the borders of it, to call them out of an element that appeared to her so dangerous and destructive[1].' In order to test the real force of nature in this matter, as distinct from experience and education, I ventured on the experiment of placing some little orphan ducklings, which had been reared away from any pond, in a shallow bath of water just deep enough for them to swim in. The experiment was two or three times repeated, but in each case with a sort of impiety, or, at any rate, gross disrespect towards the grand principle of instinct, the ducklings, instead of enjoying themselves in their appropriate element, made the most violent and unceasing efforts to escape from it. The whole theory of instinct, indeed, probably rests on a multitude of evidences which have themselves been taken for granted. At every point minute observation, or actual questioning of the facts asserted, undermines it. Addison himself must have begun to waver, before he inserted in the numbers of the 'Guardian[2]' the French philosopher's account of the ant, and its wonderful ingenuity and perseverance. Nor are passages wanting in his works, which might have been expressly written in support of the theory of development. After commenting on the various

---

[1] 'Spectator,' No. 121.   [2] Nos. 156, 157.

insensible gradations of perceptive being, 'If we look,' he says, 'into the several inward perfections of cunning and sagacity, or what we generally call instinct, we find them rising after the same manner, imperceptibly one above another, and receiving additional improvements, according to the species in which they are implanted. This progress in nature is so very gradual, that the most perfect of an inferior species comes very near to the most imperfect of that which is immediately above it.' Again: 'The whole chasm in nature, from a plant to a man, is filled up with divers kinds of creatures, rising one over another, by such a gentle and easy ascent, that the little transitions and deviations from one species to another are almost insensible;' and he quotes with approbation a passage from Locke, in which we read, 'There are some brutes that seem to have as much knowledge and reason as some that are called men[1].' Pope, who pursues much the same track in his 'Essay on Man,' permits himself to speak of 'the half-reasoning elephant.' Any one who doubts the appropriateness of such an epithet, not only to the elephant but to many other animals, should begin to study the ways and doings of the lower creatures with an eye to this very question,—at every turn asking himself how the action observed can be accounted for by a blind irrational instinct. A stumbling horse, for example, that is generally beaten for stumbling, starts after a false step before the lash is applied. How ridiculous will it be to ascribe to horses an instinct of

[1] 'Spectator,' No. 519.

starting after stumbling—a conditional instinct, that appears only in those horses that have been previously beaten when they stumbled! We need not suppose, as Lord Bacon appears to have done, that 'dogs know the dog-killer' by a kind of power of divination[1]. By their watchful habits, and quick inference from acute observation of the few particulars they are able to comprehend, it can scarcely be doubted that dogs learn something of the dispositions and intentions of mankind, recognize their humours, and distinguish those who are friendly to themselves from those who are hostile.

Numberless writers have noticed the different dispositions of the lower animals, differing not merely in separate species, but in various individuals of the same. There has been no scruple in taking the brutes themselves as types and emblems of moral qualities. Almost every vice and virtue has been unsparingly assigned to one or other of the brute creation. They are brave or cowardly, savage and treacherous, gentle and generous, industrious, idle, obedient, wayward, affectionate, malicious, working always for the common good, or full of rapacity and selfishness. It is likely enough that we often misapply these epithets, and call that courage which is only consciousness of strength, and that malignant ferocity which is really a hungry stomach and a

---

[1] 'Natural History,' § 985. 'It is a common experience that dogs know the dog-killer; when, as in times of infection, some petty fellow is sent out to kill the dogs; and that though they have never seen him before, yet they will all come forth, and bark and fly at him.'

badly-furnished larder; for such mistakes we commit also in judging of our fellow-men. But there are many beautiful instances on record in which dumb creatures have shown themselves capable beyond question of faithful friendship, and therefore as possessing at least the beginnings, if not any high advancement, of a moral nature. None perhaps is more beautiful than that told by Henry Brookes, a writer of the last century, about one of the lions in the Tower of London. A little spaniel picked up in the streets was thrown into the cage of the largest of these beasts, called for his size the king's lion. 'Immediately the little animal trembled, and shivered, and crouched, and threw itself on its back, and put forth its tongue, and held up its paws, in supplicatory attitudes, as an acknowledgment of superior power, and praying for mercy. In the meantime the lordly brute, instead of devouring it, beheld it with an eye of philosophic inspection. He turned it over with one paw, and then turned it over with the other, and smelled to it, and seemed desirous of courting a further acquaintance. From this day the strictest friendship commenced between them, a friendship consisting of all possible affection and tenderness on the part of the lion, and of the utmost confidence and boldness on the part of the dog, insomuch that he would lay himself down to sleep, within the fangs and under the jaws of his terrible patron.'

The sequel of the story is pathetic. To tell it briefly, in twelve months the little spaniel sickened and died. The lion at first supposed him to be asleep, but finding that all his efforts to awaken him were in vain, he was filled with intense anguish, would not allow the dead body to be removed, refused all sustenance or comfort, spending his time between rage and grief, till after five days of such an existence, one morning he was found dead, with his head lovingly reclined on the carcase of his little friend[1].

Were this only a fable instead of an actual incident, there is nothing in it revolting to our sense of probability, because we are perfectly aware that the lower animals constantly give indications of what in ourselves we call the moral feelings. We continually see them behaving as we ourselves behave when we submit to self-sacrifice for the sake of those we love.

We see many animals in possession of laws and constitutions answering to our own in all but one particular, namely, that theirs appear to be fixed while ours are continually changing. But most likely we overrate both the fixed character of theirs, and the instability of our own. Changes in the politics of an oyster may easily escape the notice of a man in the midst of some vast revolution (as he thinks it) of human affairs, some vast revolution which proves in the end to be nothing more than a change of names. For mankind the acquisition of language has indefinitely quickened the movement of ideas, but where language is without the aids of writing and printing, as among savage tribes, and where the language itself is an imperfect instrument

---

[1] See 'Knight's Half-Hours with the Best Authors.' No. 185: from 'The Fool of Quality.'

of thought, the same routine seems to prevail from generation to generation. Fashion in dress changes but slowly when the dress itself is nothing but a girdle; and the fashions of the mind change with as little facility when ideas and wants, and the means of expressing the one and gratifying the other, are all alike few and extremely simple.

So simple are the wants and ideas of the savage, so little above those of the elephant and the ape, that Mr. Wallace finds himself driven to the conclusion that the savage 'in his large and well-developed brain possesses an organ quite disproportionate to his actual requirements — an organ that seems prepared in advance, only to be fully utilized as he progresses in civilization.' But anything *quite disproportionate* to its actual place in nature cannot have been produced according to the theory of development. This theory therefore Mr. Wallace deems and declares inapplicable to the brain and mind of man. In support of his view he adduces several circumstances both of man's bodily and mental constitution, which he considers this theory incapable of explaining. He maintains that natural selection will not account for those rudiments of logical, moral, and æsthetic faculties which are to be found in uncivilized man; for the nakedness of the human skin, though hair upon the back would be of essential service to the unclad savage; for the absence of prehensile power from the human foot, a power which he thinks would be useful, or for those perfections of hand and voice which he thinks would be useless, to uncultivated human beings. The inference he draws 'from this class of phenomena is, that a superior intelligence has guided the development of man in a definite direction and for a special purpose, just as man guides the development of many animal and vegetable forms.'

In this illustration he overlooks the circumstance that man's selection is after all nothing more nor less than part and parcel of natural selection. In his argument from the various uses and powers of the hand and brain, which could have been of no service to men in a wild state, he neglects the consideration that what is selected through being useful in one direction may incidentally become useful in another. Had he employed his usual ingenuity on the question of man's hairless skin, he might have seen the possibility of its 'selection' through its superior beauty or the health attaching to superior cleanliness. At any rate it is surprising that he should picture to himself a superior intelligence plucking the hair from the backs of savage men, (to whom according to his own account it would have been useful and beneficial) in order that the descendants of the poor shorn wretches might, after many deaths from cold and damp, in the course of many generations take to tailoring and dabbling in bricks and mortar. In regard to the voice he makes an assertion which is surely impossible for himself or any one else to prove, namely, that 'savages certainly never choose their wives for fine voices.' But upon this assertion the whole of his argument about the voice depends. And as for the stress which he lays upon the rudimentary moral and æsthetic faculties of savages, we have shown that numbers of other animals likewise have rudimentary moral faculties, while Mr. Wallace himself makes it probable that many have a taste for colour[1], and that 'their powers of vision and their faculties of perception and emotion must be essentially of the same nature as our own[2].'

Truly in one sense every variation is prepared in advance, only to be fully utilized in the future progress of the creature that varies. Every variation, I doubt not, is so prepared in advance by a superior intelligence, but under the general laws which that intelligence has ordained, and not by a special interference. The real progress of each creature, within the spheres at least of consciousness and intelligence, would seem to consist in its growing capacity for perceiving and understanding, for entering into fellowship with, beings superior to itself. In mental powers the dog and the horse become more and more like man, the closer and the more continuous the intercourse. Could they learn our language or we theirs, the progress might be indefinitely hastened. In the general progress onwards and upwards, man, it may be believed, then first became the indisputable lord and chief over his fellow animals, when his reason had so far advanced that he could comprehend the

---

[1] 'Essays on Natural Selection,' p. 248.   [2] Ibid. p. 128.

idea of God, when his reason had grown into a capacity of hearing the divine voice, which since then, not by interference with physical conditions, but by intercourse of mind with mind, has led him forward step by step from darkness into twilight, from the twilight is still leading him forward, as his eyes become able to bear it, towards the beauty of the rosy-fingered dawn; and just as those of the lower animals are considered the most intelligent which make the most successful efforts at intercourse with man and at serving him, so, by a true analogy, may the philosopher deem those men and those races of men to be furthest on the path of enlightenment who know most of God and serve Him best.

HUMAN NATURE
AND BRUTE NATURE[1].

A poor slave, named Androcles, escaped from his master into a sandy desert. While there a lion came suddenly upon him, and by signs made him understand that it was in an agony of pain. This the slave was able to relieve by extracting a large thorn from its paw and by gentle treatment of the wound. From this time the lion shared its prey with the man, till Androcles, pining for human society, and facing even death to regain it, at length gave himself up to his master. It so happened that the slave was sent to Rome to be exposed to wild beasts at the

[1] This Essay was originally prepared as a sermon for Trinity Sunday. For the text were quoted the well-known words of 2 Peter ii. 16, 'The dumb ass, speaking with man's voice, forbad the madness of the prophet.' The design was to show that some of the most unpopular novelties in scientific opinion bore no necessary antagonism to the deepest mysteries of Christian doctrine. In regard to such an attempt it is perhaps needless to add that the kindliness of the design was not fully appreciated by those for whose benefit it was intended.

same time that the very lion which he had befriended was sent thither, among many others, to supply the cruel sports of the amphitheatre. The moment came when Androcles was to be torn in pieces. A huge famished lion rushed forth in fury upon him; then paused, crept gently towards him, and ended by fawning upon him with caressing movements. It was the lion he had known in the desert.

This is no fable, but a piece of well-known history; and the sequel is equally well-known, that the applause and admiration of all beholders at this wonderful instance of fraternity between man and beast, at this marvellous exemplification of the powers of memory and gratitude in a wild animal, secured the lives both of slave and lion.

Had this been recorded in the Hebrew Scriptures, in that noble and reverent phraseology which so often leaves out of sight all secondary causes as by comparison insignificant, and ascribes all that is good and wonderful directly to God, there can be little doubt that it would have borne a striking resemblance to the miracles wrought in favour of Elijah and Daniel; when for the one God commanded the ravens to feed him, and the ravens brought him bread and flesh in the morning and bread and flesh in the evening; and for the other God sent his angel and stopped the mouths of the lions even in their den, and they did him no hurt. Explain these miracles as you will, and the kindred one quoted by St. Peter, or accept them all without explanation as occurrences out of the course of nature and beyond our comprehension, it still follows from the language of the sacred writers that they at least supposed these brute creatures capable of intelligence, an intelligence sufficient to receive the divine commands and to avoid, so far as they might, opposition to God's will. For how else could there be any moral teaching in the circumstance that 'the dumb ass speaking with man's voice forbad the madness of the prophet?' How else can the miracle seem anything else or anything better than a piece of puerile conjuring? But this faculty, which the sacred writers therefore attribute to the brutes, the faculty of hearing and obeying the voice of God, is the basis of the highest intelligence, the basis of all true morality and religion.

That which we are now concerned to prove is, that human reason is an outgrowth and development of a faculty common to the whole animal creation; that we are the heirs of the past in fact, as we are inheritors of the future in hope; that an incalculable multitude of small advantages acquired in successive generations has brought man to his present vantage-ground of superiority; and that this very footing of advantage has now become in its turn simply the starting-point for future improvement to an estate indefinitely higher and better. It may well be impossible in a few minutes' discourse to do more than indicate the bare outline of the proof; and even this might seem inappropriate to the time and place, did we not hope to show further that these opinions, startling or even dangerous as they may seem to some, give support to high principles of humanity, and are in accordance with the course and progress of God's revelation of Himself to mankind.

It is well established that the human body in all its parts corresponds to the structure of certain of the lower animals. When first discovered this was extremely shocking to the sentiments of mankind, shocking to their pride, but shocking also to their religious sentiment, because they had been accustomed to speak of the 'human form divine,' to represent the supreme God, 'Jehovah, Jove, or Lord,' as wearing the form and acting with the members of a man, and because in the writings sacred alike to the Jew and to the Christian, they found it written that 'God created man in His own image; in the image of God created He him.' They did not stop to enquire what sort of creation was intended or what sort of likeness. They failed to observe that the vague indefinite notion they entertained of a bodily likeness was inconsistent with the Christian's cardinal doctrine of the Incarnation, according to which it is not man that wears the form of God, but God that took upon him the form of man.

It will now for a time perhaps seem equally shocking that the mind of man, which alone is left him for the divine resemblance, should notwithstanding have been developed from the mind of a brute creature, or if not developed, at any rate framed upon the same type and pattern.

A broad line has till lately been drawn between reason

and instinct, instinct appearing in a large number of instances to do or even to surpass the work of reason, but within an exceedingly limited sphere, and according to a fixed invariable course. Ingenious and thoughtful men, however, taking their opinions not from hearsay and tradition, but founding them on careful observation of the works and ways of God in nature itself, have now shown the baselessness of this ancient estimate.

The bird building its nest does not follow an invariable rule, but accommodates itself to circumstances, to the materials of the locality, to the requirements of defence, as man does with his own habitations. There is no proof that the bird builds untaught by its elders, or that it does not improve by practice. Since wasps have been known to construct their nest out of paper, itself a fabric of human invention, it is impossible they can have chosen their material by an original instinct. The cells which various bees construct attain to various degrees of perfection, and imperfections may be found in the most perfect. It has indeed been a curious fancy for men so long to entertain, that though they were created in the image of God to have dominion over the lower creatures, yet those creatures without reason, without teaching, without the God-likeness, should be able to surpass them, by a miracle or a mystery, in the accuracy or perfection of their works.

The pursuit which man in a low state of civilization has ever thought most noble is that of war. The essence of war lies in the combination of forces and the choice of opportunity. Of both these the lower animals are known to be capable. Their armies resemble human armies in following leaders, in posting sentinels, in carrying off captives, in making slaves. Creatures that are very weak combine not unfrequently to repel or to destroy an antagonist immensely too strong for their individual efforts. That rooks and other animals try, and execute justice upon, offenders against the laws and customs of their society is probable, if it cannot be absolutely proved.

The objection is sure to be urged that if the dumb animals have the progressive plastic intelligence which is thus claimed for them, it ought, in the innumerable generations which have existed, to have attained to something far higher than there is any pretence for thinking it to have done. But this objection leaves important considerations out of sight. It is true here, as in so many cases, that to him that hath shall more be given. The intelligence of man reached a point not all at once but by degrees, at which it was able to invent helps and appliances for its own benefit and improvement, and thenceforward its strides were more rapid and its distinction from lower intelligences more marked. Cancel the art of printing, cancel the signs of the alphabet, cancel the forms of articulate language, and with each one of these steps you will thrust back and degrade, not perhaps every single human intellect, but certainly the whole mass and average of human intelligence. There is no need to ask or answer the question whether thought without language is possible: without language thought cannot move, it has no grasp upon the world; it may flicker for a moment in the mind that kindles it, as a light under a bushel, but it cannot shine before men that they may see its goodness and glorify their Father in heaven. We see the proof of this in races of men that have no printed books, no symbols for writing, and but feeble imperfect languages. Civilization is wanting to them; their worship is degraded; in their habits and general morality they rise but little above the brute creation. Moreover, century after century they continue without making any apparent improvement or advance. Contrast or compare with these the lower animal creation, and it will be found, if not in its separate members, still in the whole group, not to fall so infinitely below humanity as human beings have long been pleased to imagine: for the lower animals can be taught to recognize man as their superior and friend, though his mind is beyond their comprehension, and a similar recognition is exactly what we men have to attain to in regard to God; they can be taught by pleasure and pain, motives by which we ourselves both in childhood and in age are taught, motives by which God Himself declares that He teaches us, if we are to believe His word.

That they are capable of our virtues has been shown in a notable instance; that they are capable of our follies is clear in the conspicuous vanity of the peacock; and no weakness cleaves more pertinaciously to the human mind than this of vanity, which is often found combined even with the noblest intellect. That they are influenced by feelings like ours may be learned from the gay plumage of the bird of Paradise, acquired under the same influence of the preference and admiration of others, for which fair women wear fair raiment, and for which the soldier, at extra risk to his life, is clad in scarlet.

According to a principle now well known, the earlier the period of life the greater the resemblance is likely to be between creatures akin to one another. Hence we may explain the phenomenon that some children, throughout their childhood prone to causeless mischief and stubborn resistance, become at length reasonable and self-controlled men. As for the child, so for the brute, a future of enlightened reason and self-control may be in store. The largest and most generous minds are now beginning to contemplate the possibility of an immortal destiny for all animals whatsoever. To my own mind, as doubtless to many of yours, such a conception has often seemed fanciful and ridiculous, as the greatest and best notions often do to minds that are narrow or unexpanded by a wisdom higher than their own. So it was that the gossips and philosophers of Athens mocked when they heard of the resurrection of the dead, though St. Paul was preaching only the resurrection of human beings. To extend this belief in the resurrection to all the animate creation is to extend our conception of the power and the goodness of God, to make easy many things that otherwise seem appallingly difficult in regard to His justice and His mercy. Does it seem a thing impossible with you that God should raise the dead? Is the Lord's arm shortened that it cannot save, whether it be man, or the worm that Scripture deems his fitting emblem? Or, as the Jews were jealous that the Gentiles should be saved, are we jealous that for creatures which we slaughter, trample on, enslave, and crowd out of existence, happiness and life should yet be in store as well as for ourselves?

Be willing to believe that language, reason, spiritual insight, which is the reason elevated to the capacity of knowing God—be willing to believe that these have been gradual acquisitions to humanity, and the whole course of God's Providence will at once stand out in a clearer, purer light. Supposing the soul of man thousands of years back to have been precisely what the soul of man is now, its requirements and its aptitudes must have been the same then as they are to-day, so that if the doctrine of the Trinity is essential now, it must have been essential then, when it had not been revealed. On the same supposition, too, either the record of God's will in the earliest portion of the Bible is incredibly defective, or the record of it in the completed canon of Scripture must be charged with bewildering superfluity.

But God has not dealt so with His children. He has given them their heavenly food as they were able to bear it. First by allegory and parable He unfolds His will, as a father tells his little ones the stories which they love to hear, minding ever within the stories and by means of the stories to present the truth, the lessons of the beautiful and the upright. The earliest revelation of God presents Him in the simplest form, the easiest for us to understand, as the Great Patriarch of mankind. Along with this revelation came simple commands and prohibitions, the requirements of external sacrifice, the promise and warning of temporal rewards and punishments. The law of retaliation, an eye for an eye, a tooth for a tooth, seems brutal now, but it is the beginning of a noble education. It says indeed, 'Do to others as they have done to you,' but then in regard to injuries it bids you exact no more than you have suffered, instead of taking a brutal revenge by repaying the injury tenfold: and in regard to benefits it bids you never forget to be grateful. From it springs the higher and better law, of doing to others, not as they have done to you, but as you would have them do to you. Without these beginnings the human mind could never have comprehended or received the highest education—that we are not only to forgive but to love our enemies. The system of material sacrifices trained men to a capability of understanding and of offering the sacrifice of the heart; the outward cleansings demanded by the law led them by degrees to recognize the need of inward purity. By the law came the knowledge of sin. Not till man knew that sin was sinful could he either wish for or receive a Saviour. Hence it was that Christ came not at the beginning, but only in the fulness of time. The gift of the Holy Ghost was not outpoured till men in part were ready to receive it. That it is still bestowed with so sparing a hand is not the fault of God's liberality, but of our backwardness to believe in God, to commune with Him, and thereby to grow up into His likeness. We are the mirror in which the divine image shines, if only the mirror can be made to receive the requisite brightness.

To know that sin is sinful is to become conscious of the will of God, to become conscious of a good and perfect will to which our own ought to be conformed. Not to know this will is to be still brutish; to know it only by the teaching of others is to be still among the things of a child; to know it of oneself, which is in other words to know it by the teaching of the Holy Ghost, who alone can implant the doctrine with unfailing demonstration and enable us to receive His discipline,—this at length is to be a man made in the image of God. For the fear of the Lord is the beginning of wisdom, and to depart from evil that is understanding; and to love God with all the heart and all the understanding and all the soul and all the strength, is the single aim as it is the crowning effort of the highest and purest intelligence. To be able to pray to God is the glory of reason; to do it, is the safeguard of life.

THE LAPSE OF TIME.

The divergence of opinion between scientific and unscientific persons is scarcely anywhere more conspicuous than in their measurements of the age of the world we live in. A popular impression still prevails that the old beldame earth, as Hotspur calls it, is about six thousand years of age. A little margin is sometimes allowed. By an exercise of heroic liberality a period of ten or twelve thousand years is occasionally conceded for the earth's existence. Any chronology discontented with these ample limits comes within the domain of rash and dangerous speculation. Some, indeed, who would fain conciliate all parties, are willing to extend the bounds on certain conditions. They will grant a large extra slice of time, provided that during that period the earth was a shapeless uninhabited lump, or if inhabited, not inhabited by men. 'Come, now,' says the cheap-jack, 'I'll tell you what I'll do with you; I'll throw you in another five thousand years; fifteen thousand years! and take the lot. What! not do? I'll make it twenty thousand.

Now, I'll tell you what I'll do with you: I'll make it five-and-twenty thousand years, and if that won't satisfy you, you aren't worth arguing with.'

What scientific men think of the cheap-jack's offer it is the object of this essay to consider.

The problem upon which many thoughts and speculations of science are for the moment converging is the origin of life. There are some who believe that under certain chemical conditions living creatures are continually coming into existence, ungenerated by any living parent, born as it were without birth, acquiring an animated existence, with powers of motion, feeding, and reproduction, from substances previously wanting in one or all of these capacities; such creatures, in short, as, if asked for their parentage, could but answer, each for itself, my father was an atom, and my mother a molecule. It should be remembered that the little animals supposed to arise in the manner described first become visible, if at all, as the tiniest objects that microscopes can detect. But whether there is or is not in these days a continual coming into existence of these infinitesimal pigmies, they are just such productions as the Theory of Development would suppose to have arisen originally, constituting the first outburst of life upon the globe, ancestral to the noblest forms of animated nature now extant, progenitors in an unbroken line of man himself. As a rule, among living things we find that offspring bear a tolerably exact resemblance to their parents. The lower the organism the less easy is it to distinguish specimens of one generation from those of another; and even in the most highly organized creatures the points of resemblance generally far outweigh the points of difference between the parents and their children. In short, under ordinary circumstances, not one generation only, but a hundred, may pass away without registering any perceptible alteration in the character of a species. A hundred generations of mankind would require a period of about three thousand years. A hundred generations of less important creatures might not perhaps require even as large a number of hours. But between the two extremes the necessary periods would bear a kind of ratio to the perfection of the organism. Variations might now and then follow one another in quick succession, and then a pause come of a thousand generations or so before any further changes in the character of a species.

Such are the conditions under which Mr. Darwin and his followers believe it possible for the whole sequence of changes to have been effected, which have ended in peopling the whole earth with a countless variety of the most diverse forms of life. Many persons are horrified at the notion of linking together a man and a monkey even by the most distant ties of consanguinity; what will they say to a genealogy which begins with an almost invisible speck and ends with a Patagonian giant — a genealogy which asserts that, through the slow process of minute changes occurring for the most part at rare intervals, our fair humanity has been developed or evolved out of creatures which no unaided human eye could distinguish from the dust on which we carelessly trample. To some ears such a theory must sound wild and preposterous beyond all the boundaries of sane and rational thinking. And, in truth, no censure could be too severe, no ridicule too keen for so extravagant a piece of folly as this theory must be, if the old and still prevailing notions about the age of the world have any foundation in fact. It only begins to be reasonable, if we can afford to stretch our notions of history from the narrow margin of six thousand to the broader field of six hundred thousand years, with an indefinite past in the background.

This vast lapse of time, as commensurate with the existence of the inhabited globe, is essential to the Theory of Development. It must be established, as it has been, by independent evidence of its own, before it can give to that theory its absolutely necessary support. But the Theory of Development in its turn helps the mind to believe and realize this enormous lapse of time, with its seemingly never-ending march and flow, rank upon rank, wave upon wave, by finding work and employment for all its almost measureless duration. It explains, as it were, why the drama of life still goes on, why the play was not long ago played out, and the curtain let fall upon all the busy multitudinous actors.

Time of itself does nothing; but nothing can be done without time. It is not a personal agent, but a necessary condition. We cannot even think, much less reason, of things as occurring out of time and independently of it, any more than we can think or reason of matter as existing independent of space. Every occurrence takes time: and yet we may not leap from this fact to the conclusion that a countless multitude of occurrences will require a vast duration of time. Professor Tyndal, in his Lecture on the Scientific Use of the Imagination, refers to waves of light less than $\frac{1}{30000}$ of an inch in length. How many do you suppose of such waves would be required to compass a mile? How many to accomplish the 185,000 miles which light travels in a second? Each undulation is a separate occurrence, so that we have millions of millions of occurrences following one upon another in a second of time. In studying, therefore, the complete fabric of the globe, or even of the whole material universe as far as it comes within our ken, the problem for solution is not whether these great results could or could not have been brought to pass in an indefinitely short space of time, in the twinkling of an eye, as one might say, but whether the space of time employed in their production has actually and in fact been indefinitely short or indefinitely long. We ought also to bear in mind that the terms we use when we speak of *long* and *short*, are relative not absolute—relative to the duration of our own lives, or to some other arbitrary standard which we are pleased to set up for purposes of comparison. Thus a year is long compared with a minute, but short compared with a millennium; a thousand years would be an enormous length for the life of a mortal man, but compared with the ceaseless flow of ages, which we call eternity, this same thousand years becomes, as it were, an imperceptible speck, less than a drop of water compared to the Atlantic, a point of time so inconceivably minute, that no human mind could grasp it as an intelligible unit of measurement. For time, we have an inexhaustible past on which to draw. Against any given theory of production, no objection pure and simple that the theory makes too large a demand upon time, can be maintained. An objection, to be valid against the existence of life on the earth a million of years back, must postulate that there was no earth then in existence, or none capable of supporting life; for if we choose to stand by the doctrine of final causes, life upon the earth must have begun as soon as life upon the earth was possible, otherwise we should have a fair and perfect design with its purpose unaccomplished; or, if we prefer the Theory of Development carried out to its legitimate consequences, equally must we admit, that as soon as the earth was fitted for living creatures, living creatures would be generated upon it.

In tracing back the duration of the globe, the first demand of the uninitiated will be for the written evidence of historical records. The popular impression claims to be founded upon such evidence of the most authoritative description. Little do the upholders of this impression in general understand that they are building their faith, not upon the Book of Genesis, or the inspiration of the Hebrew lawgiver, but on the arithmetical speculations of an Irish archbishop, who lived in the seventeenth century.

Before we can accept the Hebrew genealogies as competent data for historical chronology, we must understand the principles on which they were framed. In ancient languages we have abundant evidence to show that the ties of blood were not as sharply distinguished as among ourselves. The same word sufficed to designate son and grandson, and even the most remote descendant. A man's heir was called his son; an usurping successor might receive the same title [1]; and, beyond all this, it has been shown to have been 'a common practice with the Jews to distribute genealogies into divisions, each containing some favourite or mystical number; and that, in order to do this, generations were either repeated or left out.' Some persons, perhaps, will say, 'We don't believe it, or we don't believe it in regard to any of the biblical genealogies.' And yet the very first chapter of the New Testament is the most conclusive and incontrovertible proof of the statement; for our Lord's genealogy [2] is there expressly divided into three periods of fourteen generations each, and the middle period has been stripped of three generations in order to bring it down to the pre-determined number. The

---

[1] As in the inscription 'Jehu, the son of Omri,' referred to by Lord A. C. Hervey, in Smith's Dict. of the Bible, Art. 'Genealogy.'

[2] Smith's Dictionary of the Bible, Art. 'Genealogy of Jesus Christ,' Lord A. C. Hervey, referring to Dr. Mill. Compare also Hengstenberg, Genuineness of the Pentateuch, vol. ii. p. 294, Translation, 1847.

names of three well-known princes (Ahaziah, Joash, Amaziah), whose histories occupy several chapters in the Second Book of Kings, are omitted, and Amaziah's son is described, without further note or comment, as a son begotten by one who was really his father's great-grandfather. In a matter so obvious, there cannot attach to the compiler of the genealogy the very faintest suspicion of bad faith. He was following the custom of his country, for reasons then deemed, and perhaps in those days actually being, good and sufficient. Can we make as satisfactory an apology for men in the present day, who shut their eyes to the nature of the evidence on which they build opinions about the age of the world opposed to the discoveries of science? If in the first century of the Christian era, in times of comparative enlightenment, by men of approved truth and uprightness, genealogies could be compiled without the smallest regard being paid to the actual number of successive generations, it becomes impossible to attach any value as chronological evidence to Hebrew genealogies fifteen hundred, or, for all that we can tell, fifteen thousand years more ancient. Had the genealogy on which this conclusion rests admitted a chance of error, had there been any motive for fraud in its construction, did any suspicion lie against its authenticity, the case would be weakened. But just because there neither was nor could have been error in the mind of the writer, or deceit in his intention, just because what he wrote, he wrote deliberately and of set purpose, it is certain that his record is not, and was never meant to be, a measure of time; and that those who persist in measuring time by similar records, are the victims of a manifest delusion, ensnared, it may be feared in too many cases, with their eyes open.

There is an old jest that, in the pride of antiquity, a Welshman generally traces back his lineage not only as far as Adam, but a great deal further. Nothing was easier, before the age of historical criticism, than for men or nations, whose real origin was lost in obscurity, to link their names to an illustrious past. Nothing was easier than to develope the obscurity itself into a long line of remote ancestors, whose names and virtues could be invented and multiplied at pleasure. What the poet was only too willing to imagine, the mathematician seemed able to confirm, by registering astronomical occurrences in far-distant long-past ages with as much precision as those which he predicted, and predicted truly, for his own and future times. The Hindoo chronology reckons the age of the world by millions of years. The Egyptians twenty centuries ago used to tell of 330 kings of whom they knew no more than the names. There were Greeks who claimed to be older than the moon; others who anticipated the theory of *abiogenesis* by claiming to be sprung from the earth itself without the intervention of parents; and yet others, who with more modesty or more pride, as we please to regard it, derived their origin from gods and demigods. None were willing to be thought new people. The man of yesterday, the *novus homo*, the upstart, the parvenu, has ever been disliked and laughed at by society. And in like manner, among nations, a new rival excites the fears and encounters the ridicule of the established clique. Claims to antiquity, therefore, were as advantageous to possess as they were easy to forge. Those that have been mentioned, being unattested by any corroborative facts, and, where they are not obviously false, being unsusceptible of proof, are worthless in themselves. One thing they tend to show, namely, that all remembrance of the real origin of mankind, and of the date of that origin, had been absolutely lost to those ancient peoples. From over the sea, from beyond the mountains, from the bright east or the frozen north, they might know that their forefathers had made pilgrimage in distant ages—or they might know of no time, however far back, when the seat of their habitation had not been occupied by their own progenitors. In either case their ignorance of primeval history is as absolute as it is conspicuous. One prevailing tradition, it is true, is current alike in sacred and profane literature, of a far-off golden time, an age of simplicity, when man conversed with the beasts of the field, when the earth brought forth her fruits spontaneously, with her bosom as yet unvexed by the ploughshare, ere the knowledge or the discrimination of good and evil had come into the world—the record, in one word, as all these details tend to prove, of a time before man had become a moral being; a dim mysterious recollection, almost like a dream, of a time before the animal nature had been decisively exalted into humanity.

Some persons believe, against all probability of evidence, that spoken language was a sudden original inspiration instead of a gradual invention. None, however, assert the right of believing the same thing in regard to letters or written language. The progressive origin of alphabetical signs is admitted on all sides, so that there must have been a time when man had to trust to his fallible memory instead of written memoranda. The growth of picture-writing itself must have been extremely slow, from the difficulty of establishing an agreement as to the meaning of particular representations. What this difficulty amounts to may to some extent be tested any day in a picture-gallery, where all the appliances and skill of modern art are at our service. Without the aid of a descriptive catalogue, it is but seldom that any two accounts of the meaning of the same picture would be found to agree. The art of drawing, it may well be supposed, was not an inspiration. It had to be invented. The very idea of transmitting a record to future ages would only occur with the advance of civilization. The crumbling surface of the rock, the decaying bark of trees, would be the first perishable and soon obliterated manuscripts. Before account could be taken of months and years, astronomy must have made some progress. Before the flow of centuries could be accurately noted, arithmetic must have advanced far beyond the stage at which we still find it among numerous savage nations. An Esquimaux couple, it is said, find it difficult to count their own children, even when they are no more than four or five[1].

From these considerations alone we may feel perfectly certain that numbers of ages elapsed before men acquired the means of recording the duration of time by any definite measurements. Unconsciously and without set purpose, perhaps the very earliest tribes and the most untutored have left behind them traces not only of their existence but of the date and era at which they lived; traces which we are only now beginning to decipher, and to read with faltering lips.

All around us in England, in Devonshire, in Torquay, and all over the globe, lie the memorials of human beings, of whose day and generation the oldest historical records we possess know absolutely nothing. Here and there the tale is told by a heap of shells. From such heaps we know what dishes were served at the Dane's dinner-table, at a time when cereal crops were unknown in Denmark, and sea-weed was used instead of salt[2]. Oysters and cockles, mussels and periwinkles, seem to have been *ad libitum;* the stag, the roe-deer, and the wild boar were at the service of that ancient Dane as often as he could catch them with his weapons of wood, stone, horn, or bone[3]; when pork and venison were scarce, his palate could content itself with dog or fox. From the waters of the mountain-lake, from the centre of the high-piled barrow, in the circles

---

[1] Sir J. Lubbock, 'Prehistoric Times,' p. 502, second edition.
[2] Ibid. p. 223.   [3] Ibid. p. 233.

of giant stones upon broad-stretching plain or wild moorland, from peat-moss and railway-cutting and limestone cavern, we obtain, as Sir John Lubbock and Mr. Pengelly and others have so well shown, the unwritten records of prehistoric man, of human beings unnoticed in any credible history, and preceding all well-established definite historical dates whether of sacred or profane literature. Who reared the Titanic monuments of Stonehenge and Abury we know not. We know not who constructed the extraordinary animal-mounds of Wisconsin in North America—mounds hundreds of feet long, reared a few feet above the level plains, in the figures of men and beasts and birds and reptiles. These monuments, if such they were intended to be, must have demanded prodigious industry for their construction. They imply a considerable population, and some advance in artistic skill. But why they were designed, and who designed them, are circumstances alike unknown. It is necessary to press home this argument founded upon our ignorance, and to dwell upon it with some emphasis, because numbers of persons are pleased to imagine and assert that, within two or three thousand years before the Christian era, the whole human population of the globe was as it were still in the bud, and that from a single family, not mustering a dozen members to start with, all its tribes have since then been derived, with their endless diversities of features, hair, complexion, customs, tastes, and other qualities both of mind and body. According to the old chronology we are to suppose that within this limited space of time, from under a single roof, the children went forth, spreading over all lands, not only miraculously forgetting the common ancestral language, but forgetting the arts, the traditions, the sentiments, which they had in common, retrograding in some cases into a savage ferocity or an almost imbecile simplicity, in others retaining or developing forms of an advanced civilization. Esquimaux and Hottentots, Japanese and Red Indians, the Negro and the Greek, are thus united in ties of cousinship by no means remote. Arts, monuments, and modes of life essentially different in spirit and character are supposed, within these narrow bounds of time, to have sprung up; nor only to have sprung up, but to have passed away, leaving only a few faint vestiges to recall the artists, the heroes, the lawgivers, the national temper, the genius of the time, whereunto they owed their existence. It must surely be allowed that marriage customs change with slow reluctance; an alteration of the sentiment with which women are regarded is not easily or quickly produced. Yet on no subject are the practices and opinions of mankind more widely diversified. One wife to one husband is in some places the rule; but in others, one husband to many wives, one wife to many husbands, or husbands and wives without any special appropriation, which some societies consider a selfish infringement of the general right. According to the customs of different nations, wives must be fought for, or stolen, or purchased, or caught in a race, or wooed and won with pin-money and other endearments. According to the feeling of different races, the wife is a chattel, a beast of burden, a slave, a stewardess, a domestic ornament, an equal, or a master[1]. Let it be granted that many of these customs and sentiments may have been contemporaneous in their growth or development, the same thing cannot be admitted of the different centres of colonization in which they grew and developed. Men do not without cause quit their ancestral homes to found colonies in remote parts of the world; and the causes only arise at intervals. When the cause has arisen, and the new settlement been occupied, the exiles retain for the most part, and long retain in affectionate remembrance the manners and customs, the religion and laws, of the mother-country; or when the remembrance is other than affectionate, they retain them from the want of an alternative, from the conservatism in which all men to a greater or less degree participate, from the incapacity of the human mind to strike out new customs, or revolutionize ideas, except by a gradual and half-unconscious progression.

Among the visible and tangible proofs of man's and the earth's antiquity, few are more interesting than those presented in the section, well known to geologists, cut by the railway through the delta of the Tinière, a torrent flowing into the Lake of Geneva[2]. Three layers of vegetable soil appear in the section, at depths of four and ten and nineteen feet respectively below the

---

[1] See chapter on Marriage, in Sir J. Lubbock's 'Origin of Civilization.'

[2] Sir J. Lubbock, 'Prehistoric Times,' p. 380; Sir C. Lyell, 'Antiquity of Man,' p. 27.

present surface. These layers contained distinctive relics. In the first were found ' Roman tiles and a coin,' in the second ' fragments of unvarnished pottery, and a pair of tweezers in bronze;' in the third, ' fragments of rude pottery, pieces of charcoal, broken bones, and a human skeleton having a small, round, and very thick skull.' The thick-headed owner of that skull is computed to have lived, at the lowest estimate, about five thousand years ago. But the cone of the delta began to be formed long before the man was buried in it, and higher up the stream another cone is found about twelve times as large, requiring therefore a time for its formation about twelve times as long, unless we have recourse to that miserable refuge for the destitute in argument, which consists in supposing that causes now slow and comparatively regular, operated in former times with an incomparably greater speed and a more spasmodic violence, of which no trace remains, nor likelihood appears in the record. In a word, we may infer that, so far from the shapely order and decorous arrangement of the earth's surface being only six thousand years old, it has taken no less than fifty or a hundred thousand years to pile up this one little heap of mud and gravel. The age of human works buried under the fertilizing sediment of the stately Nile is much disputed, but there can be little doubt, if we take into consideration the ancient fluviatile deposits in terraces sometimes hundreds of feet above the present alluvial plain, that the long-unknown sources of the mysterious river have produced ten myriad repetitions of the annual overflow, pouring down its waters to the sea through a thousand centuries[1].

But Egypt and Switzerland are a long way off; geologizing in a railway-cutting has been before now a fatal employment; and digging pits forty feet deep into the mud of the Nile is an operation attended with difficulties peculiar to itself. Here, however, in Torquay, close at hand, we possess a register of time as compact, as accessible, as genuine, as the Library of the British Museum. Limestone, it is well known, is formed beneath the waters of the sea. When it appears above the sea-level, it must have been upheaved from its ocean-bed. How long a period must be allowed for the hill which contains Kent's cavern to have been formed by this double process, may be left for the present to the imagination. How long a time elapsed before the cavern was burst open or eaten out from the solid limestone, we will not enquire. Thanks to the diligent exploration of it; thanks to the unwearied courtesy of its scientific curators[2], the contents of the cavern, or at least a portion of them, are now well known. Not only do they embrace the remains of animals not now existing in England, but they embrace the remains of animals long since lost to the globe. With these are mingled the products of human intelligence, the weapons of the savage. The cave-earth which, as well as the stalagmite, contains these relics of a most remote

---

[1] Lyell, 'Elements of Geology,' p. 118, ed. 1865.

[2] Messrs. Pengelly and Vivian, resident at Torquay, acting members of the distinguished committee of exploration.

antiquity, is itself permeated with films of stalagmite, a conclusive proof of its gradual introduction. Over the lower portions have been formed in succession three solid stalagmitic floors, remnants of which have quite lately been discovered still imbedded in the cavern [1]. Let us for a moment consider what this implies. If we transport ourselves to Matlock Bath in Derbyshire, for the small fee of a penny, any one of its 'petrifying wells'[2] will be open to our inspection. In these curious grottoes whatever object you please, natural or artificial, be it skull or the cap that once covered it, be it basket or bird, or shell or leaf, may be encrusted with a coating of stalagmite. The inexperienced visitor would like to place an object in the well, and to wait while the 'petrifying' waters do their work. He is surprised to find that in that case he must wait and watch for months and years, while the slow persevering stream falls upon his treasure with its ceaseless drip, drip, drip, and that the work so slowly accomplished would not be accomplished at all if the flowing of the stream were hastened. Imagine, then, in this famous cavern of ours what an interminable song, though an intermittent one, must have been sung with this drip, drip, drip, through ages and ages, to produce, as in one place it has done, a solid stalagmitic mass full twelve feet in thickness. Now, according to Usher's chronology, we have seventeen centuries from Adam to the Flood, and twenty-

---

[1] See Reports of British Association, 1868, p. 57, and 1869, p. 199, by W. Pengelly, Esq., F.R.S.

[2] This is the popular name for them. They do not petrify the specimens placed in them, but only coat them with stalagmite.

three centuries from the Flood to the age of Julius Cæsar. If this chronology is to be accepted, Kent's cavern must have been filled either in the first period or in the second. As the same arguments will apply to each, let us assume that the second or longer period sufficed for this purpose, and see what further admissions this assumption will involve. We have three and twenty centuries at our disposal. At the end of that time we know historically that Britain was occupied by tribes more or less savage, some of them going about almost naked, destitute of almost all the arts of civilization. We are to imagine the ancestors of this wild race migrating from Asia and slowly pioneering their way to the western limits of Europe. Necessity is the mother of invention; but these men in their difficult adventurous travel through unknown seas and pathless jungles tenanted by dangerous beasts, learn only how to forget. They forget the use of brass and iron, and take to weapons and tools of flint; they give up tillage; they give up building strong towers, and shelter themselves in wooden huts or caves and dens of the earth. The climate of Western Asia is warm and sunny, that of England often, and in many parts, bleak and foggy and cold; therefore these intelligent children of Noah, in order perhaps to harden themselves in the process of acclimatization, as they force their way into the fog and mist, instead of keeping or assuming the flowing robes of the Asiatic, exchange their garments, at any rate in battle, for a wash of paint. How interesting it would be to have the family portraits of a

Highland clan from the earliest times, showing how they gradually made it fashionable to do without the various articles of clothing which one by one they have been induced to resume[1]! During the same epoch, within the same limits of time, migrating also from the warm regions of Asia, came elephants and lions, hyenas and bears, the rhinoceros and the elk. Little recked they then of change of climate, which now they so ill endure. They prowled all over Europe; they swam across the English Channel. Yet before the historical period begins in Gaul and Britain, most of these species had had time not only to make their way thither, not only to flourish and abound in these habitations, but to die out and to be forgotten. We know for certain that elephants once roamed over Devon. Did they succumb to the flint weapons of the savage? Was the same savage able to extirpate the hyena and the lion, though the representatives of those fierce beasts still partially set us at defiance in India, notwithstanding

---

[1] The resuming process has not yet been adopted by the modern Fuegians, for Dr. Hooker informs us that at the extreme south of Tierra del Fuego, and in mid-winter, he has often seen the men lying asleep in their wigwams, without a scrap of clothing, and the women standing naked, and some with children at their breasts, in the water up to their middles gathering limpets and other shell fish, while the snow fell thickly on them and on their equally naked babies.'—Sir J. Lubbock, 'Prehistoric Times,' p. 532. Jerome declares that he had himself seen the Attacotti, a British tribe, eating human flesh. See Gibbon (vol. iii. p. 270, ed. 1854), who in several passages refers to the practice among various British tribes of going naked, especially in war, citing Appian, Ammianus, and Giraldus Cambrensis as his authorities for British customs. It will be remembered that Cæsar speaks even of the Southern Britons as fighting ' omnibus membris expediti.'

the rifles and gunpowder of modern civilization? Let us imagine that within the specified time all that has been mentioned could have happened, and that some of the animals, such as the woolly rhinoceros, had time to assume the characters of northern species, or that the climate had time for vast changes and alterations, or that the winds perhaps in those days blew hot and cold with the same breath so as to suit arctic and tropical species indifferently;—we must imagine further that within the same limits the three floors of stalagmite could have been formed in succession, and two of them successively broken up. They must have been formed, not during the whole of the period, but only during that part of it which *followed* the introduction into Britain of wild beasts, and of men who used flint weapons; for one unmistakeable weapon of human manufacture, and innumerable bones of the great old cave bear have been found within the rock-like breccia of stone and stalagmite and cave-earth, some feet below both the floors of more recent formation[1]. The longer the period, therefore, we allow for the migration from the East and the dying out of civilized life, the shorter is the period left for the stalagmitic formation. Yet probably the whole twenty-three centuries would not suffice for the formation of one of the floors; how much less could a fraction of the period suffice to form all three, and to supply the intervals during which, through some change of

---

[1] 'Report of British Association, 1869,' p. 201.

circumstances, the cave-earth was accumulating, and consequently no solid floor being formed.

At Matlock the drip is continuous, being supplied by a stream, and not being, as in Kent's cavern, dependent on the chances of the rainfall and the quantity of water that may percolate through a limestone roof. At Matlock, for purposes of trade, it is an object that a coating of stalagmite should be formed as quickly as possible. With this view the water is allowed to fall at the rate of fifty or sixty drops a minute, the drip being maintained at numerous points simultaneously. At Matlock we may roughly estimate that an inch of stalagmite would require four years for its formation, so that twelve feet and a half would require six hundred years. In Kent's cavern, on the other hand, the drip is often interrupted. There is no commercial interest at hand to regulate the speed in the most advantageous manner, so that it falls sometimes too quickly and sometimes too slowly. The points at which it falls are few and far between. It cannot reasonably be supposed in any year to produce even a twentieth of the effect we have estimated for the drip at Matlock. In other words, the two later floors of the cavern would alone require a period of twelve thousand years for their formation. Even at this rate the cavern would probably have been so extremely damp and uncomfortable that no men or beasts would have chosen it for a shelter in rainy weather.

But the cavern inscriptions make it as certain as can be that the rate of speed here allowed for the formation of stalagmite is vastly too high, and therefore that the time allowed for the formation is vastly too low. The famous inscription of 1688 was shown to me a few days back[1]. It was at that very time wet with the drip from the cavern roof, a drip falling at the rate of thirty-four drops a minute. If the date were really cut in the year 1688 (and there is no reason to suppose that it was not), by our first calculation more than two inches of stalagmite ought to have formed over it. Instead of which there is but a thin veneer, a veneer that was observed upon it more than forty years ago, and which has not in all those forty years increased enough to make such a description of it inappropriate. If the date 1615 be authentic, over which, in the opinion of the superintendents of the exploration, not one-eighth of an inch of stalagmite has been formed in more than two centuries and a-half, at the same rate of progression twelve feet and a-half of stalagmite would demand for its formation three hundred thousand years.

This cavern by itself, therefore—this one little crack in the outermost rind of the earth's surface—proves a comparatively immense antiquity for the existence of organic life and of human beings upon the globe. But to compare the antiquity of the cavern contents with the antiquity of the limestone formation in which they are contained is positively beyond any intelligible numerical measurement. Yet the limestone formation itself is filled with the relics of living creatures, and in some

[1] Nov. 21, 1870.

parts, if not in all, is one gigantic mass of such remains.

In cliffs of sea-shore and river, in railway-cuttings, in mine-shafts and quarries, we may often see layers of the earth's crust in the order of their original deposition. Except where the signs are present of some subsequent violent interference, this order is uniform and invariable. It is not that all the members of the series are invariably present, far from it; but in order of deposition the relations of higher and lower are never interchanged. Every one of the many different layers which have been distinguished by geologists has a distinctive group of fossils. You may, if you please, suppose that for each of these layers of the earth's crust there was a new creation of living creatures, wonderfully like at each successive step, though wonderfully different at long intervals, as though they were the work of an artist whose ideas moved but slowly; but for such a supposition you have no authority; the conception has neither simplicity nor grandeur; it does not even accord with the facts, since, amid the general change of organic structures, we find the permanence of a few; and while the groups of two successive layers have, each of them, numerous distinctive forms, it is impossible to draw any definite boundary-line between the groups themselves, which sometimes intermingle with an inextricable interlacing on their confines. Nothing comes out more clearly to the student of the rocks, than that the world of to-day is the world of millions of years back; from one point of view ever-changing, yet ever essentially the same; from another point of view, out of the utmost regularity of alternation, never producing the same thing, or presenting the same aspect twice. We think that the stage has been essentially altered, because in the days of that immeasurable past *we* did not strut upon it. We are unable to fathom the depth of our own insignificance, and are unwilling to believe in a march of time, compared with which the span of our own lives seems so contemptible. In the depths of the ocean the formation of chalk is said to be going on at this very day. Probably there is no time known to the geologist at which the formation of chalk has not been going on in the depths of the ocean; but its older layers have been altered by chemical and mechanical forces, by fire, by pressure, and by other means.

We know that chalk and limestone do not form in the open air. If we find them piled up in enormous hills and mountains high above the level of the sea, and far from its coasts, we know that they did not grow in that position; that once their proud crests and ridges lay low in an ocean bed. They could not have been formed on a sudden, or rapidly, or by any other than the slow steps of infinitesimally small successive accumulations: for we find them filled throughout with the evidences of life, shells and sponges, and corals of exquisite beauty and delicacy, generations after generations of which must have had time to build up their beautiful fabrics. Many things may be hastened; you may quicken the growth of many; but you can't hurry a sponge. Every foot and inch of a chalk cliff, of a limestone mountain, must have been formed originally under water with almost incredible slowness. It must have been raised up to meet the clouds of heaven since its formation in the ocean-depth. Do you think that this can have been a rapid process? Volcanic cones, it is true, are sometimes piled up by a sudden effort. But with widespread platforms of solid rock the upheaving forces deal more respectfully. An average elevation of a foot or two in a century, is perhaps a high exceptional speed for such movements. But this rate requires a thousand centuries for a hill only one or two thousand feet high, to rise, not from the depths, but from the surface of the water. If we had only a single formation to deal with instead of scores of them; if we had a thickness of only one thousand feet of the earth's crust to consider, instead of scores of thousands, the proved antiquity of the globe would be enormous. What is to be said, then, when we stand face to face with what geologists have been pleased to call the new red sandstone? This formation cannot be less than millions of years old, although in relation to the Devonian limestone it is indisputably new. Those deep red rocks, that with their fantastic profiles in so many places fringe the southern border of Devon, must have been formed since the limestone; for the simple reason, that in every part they are full of pebbles or fragments of the limestone containing characteristic fossils of the earlier formations. It will at least be granted that you cannot break off a piece from a rock before the rock itself exists. Prior, then, to the very beginning of the formation of these red conglomerates, the limestone rock must have been formed; it must have been heaved up above the level of the sea; fragments must have been broken off from it, rolled into pebbles, triturated into sand. As the breaking, and the rolling, and the grinding went on, so with equal steps would the growth of the conglomerate proceed. But the workshop and the work must still have been beneath the waters of the ocean, and not till the whole work of formation was finished could the further process be begun of raising the work above the level of the waves.

It is not uncommon to find fossils in the pebbles of a conglomerate rock showing lines of a dislocating fracture filled with spar. The fossil shell or coral once had an inhabitant. We must allow time for its life and death. Its vacant tabernacle must then have become filled with extraneous matter. This must have required time to harden into rock. While that rock was still in the mass, some cause must have operated to fracture it, and such causes are not of every-day operation. After this, more time was needed to fill up the divisional line with spar; more time to break off the fragment containing the shell from the general mass of the rock; more time to roll it into a pebble; more time to imbed it hard and fast in a conglomerate rock; more time to raise the rock high out of the waters; and, lastly, one more vast addition of time for the crumbling away of the conglomerate formation, so as to .expose the tall sea-cliff from which human hands might gather this memorial relic of untold ages.

The same tale is told by the coal-measures. Dr. Dawson, of Montreal, has drawn out the argument from the carboniferous formation[1] with extraordinary force and a convincing plainness that leaves nothing to be desired, for the benefit of any one who will read his great work on Acadian geology. The formation of coal depends on sub-aërial growths, affected by sub-aqueous action. The trees and plants, out of which coal is formed, for the most part could not possibly have grown under water. The mud, the sand, the stone which cover seams of coal, could not have been laid over them without the agency of water to bring them down, and spread them out in regular layers of stratification. When the hollow bark of a tall tree is found erect upon its roots, with those roots still permeating the clay from which they once drew nourishment, it is evident that time must be allowed for the growth of the tree, for the almost complete decay which left nothing of it but its bark and roots, and for the slow accumulation of sediment which has encased without overthrowing it. A complete alteration must have taken place in the conditions of the ground in the interval between the time when the tree began to grow, and the time when a length of seven or eight feet of its upright stem was buried in mud. Layers, indeed, of sand and mud may be spread out over small areas by storms and inundations with comparative speed; but if above the sands we come to thicknesses of limestone composed almost

---

[1] A formation later than the Devonian, and earlier than the New Red Sandstone.

entirely of animal remains, such as those of shells and fish, not only are we forced to admit a long period for the successive generations of those creatures, but we are forced to observe the products of the ocean lying actually above the products of the dry land, as though, according to the old poetical extravagance, the stag and doe had taken to the waters and the fishes been building in the tree-tops. The conclusion is inevitable, that what was once dry land, fruitful in vegetation, in process of time became a swamp, and from the swamp became a sea. It will be a fresh surprise, but a fresh evidence of time's duration, if above the limestone we find more clay with more plants buried in more mud, and over-topped by more limestone. Bearing in mind the old supposition, that order and beauty and life upon the globe are only six thousand years' old, astonishment should reach its climax when we find, as we do, that within the thickness of only a few feet of the earth's crust, the record that we have been describing is repeated again and again and again; but beyond the climax, a fresh and overpowering marvel awaits us, when, as at one spot in British America, the record expands itself from a few feet into sixteen thousand, showing conclusively by eighty successive bands of coal that fourscore times at least, and perhaps many more, while that thickness of the earth's crust was forming, the waters gave place to dry land, and in turn the dry land to the waters,—showing conclusively that during all the period of these changes tall forests of graceful trees abounded on the globe, along with exquisite ferns and curious reptiles, and beetles and winged insects of great size and beauty; while fish replenished the waters, along with an infinity of shells and corals, and other inhabitants of the deep. Yet these sixteen thousand feet, these eighty successive forests, these hundred and sixty changes, comprise but a small fraction of the whole known succession of strata.

It is true that different strata not only may, but must have been forming at one and the same time in different parts of the world. But when one stratum has been formed out of the wreck of another, it is self-evident that they cannot have been formed together. The same thing is obvious in regard to any number of layers found lying in undisturbed succession one above the other. They must have been formed successively, the lowest first, the highest last. But one point about them is far from obvious, namely, the length of the interval that may have intervened between the end of one formation and the beginning of another. The great African desert has been the great African desert as far back as human histories extend; yet in times geologically recent it lay beneath the waters of the ocean. Should it be again submerged before any fertilizing agencies have covered it with signs of its sub-aërial exposure, another layer of sand may be thrown down upon it, containing new marine fossils, and no memorial be left to the future geologist of the vast era during which its kindly influence was warming the winds of Europe, and saving us from a glacial climate. The ground you stand on is passing through such an interval. It was under the sea once; doubtless it will be under the sea again in the future. Look into that future; look into that past. Can you measure either of those intervals in the years of common chronology? Yet all over the world the succession of geological strata proclaims the recurrence over and over again of such intervals; silent, indeed, as to positive evidence, but widening the possible limits of time's duration to the furthest stretch of fancy.

All our great continents have been ever so many times, either in the mass or piecemeal, under the waves of the ocean. Nothing hinders that the bed of every great ocean should have been ever so many times turned into dry land. This interchange is going on now in numberless regions of sea and land. All the facts as we find them are such as they might be expected to be had this interchange been going on, as no doubt it has been, through an indefinite past. We are bound to allow millions of years for the formation of the strata that have been already examined. There may be depths below the lowest depths yet explored by geologists; there have certainly been immense intervals which have left no materials for the geologist to explore; and when all the profoundest deep of stratification shall have been explored, we may still find that the record of all these unnumbered millions of years is but, as it were, the latest page of the volume—a page that may have been preceded by a thousand others now almost irrevocably lost or become utterly illegible. There is nothing to hinder the supposition that those earlier pages, if they existed, were, amidst innumerable differences, still in their general aspect very like the latest, as long or longer, as full of the memorials of eventful circumstance, of constant change dominated by and springing from the operation of unchanging laws. As the time is absolutely incalculable which the theory of evolution requires to account for the highest forms of life upon the earth, so the time which all these considerations leave open for the work is absolutely beyond calculation. The theory cannot ask for more than the facts make it possible to offer.

We hear men sometimes dwell on an expression which they fancy to be Scriptural, 'that there should be time no longer[1];' as if time by any possibility could ever come to an end! It is a pity that they should completely misinterpret the passage on which their opinion fancies itself to be grounded. It is a still greater pity that they should use the language of rational human beings, without being at the pains to determine whether their words have any intelligible meaning: for certainly to the human mind any beginning or end of time is wholly inconceivable. Language itself will not bear with the conception, unless it be consistent to speak of a *time* when time was not, of a *time* when time will be no more.

There is a poem, and a sweet one, by the present Poet-Laureate, in which the murmuring brook is made to speak the language of the moralist, and to proclaim the transitory nature of all human affairs, by a com-

[1] Revelation x. 6, Authorised Version.

parison between the short duration of man's life and its own unceasing current—

> 'For men may come, and men may go,
> But I flow on for ever.'

Such is the proud language of the murmuring brook. Yet the boast is an untrue one; for if any conclusion in regard to the future can be warranted from the facts of the past, none can be more sure than that no particular brook will flow on for ever. Instead of a brook, it may become a mighty river like the St. Lawrence; it may dash over precipitous cliffs with a vaster fall and volume than Niagara; and, after all, the slow inexorable changes of the earth's crust will one day make its flow impossible, and the channel of it shall know its stream no more. Only the flow of time is unending, of time which does nothing, but out of or without which nothing can be done, — of time, replete with glorious wonders as far back as the knowledge or the imagination of man can penetrate, through every age, through every million of years that can be rescued from forgetfulness, bearing fresh testimony, in the greatness and the endlessness of the work, to the eternal power and wisdom of the Supreme Worker.

NOTE ON THE HYPOTHESIS

OF

SPONTANEOUS GENERATION.

PRESUMING that there is not a particle of evidence as yet established in favour of the supposition known as the doctrine of *abiogenesis*, it does not follow that no such evidence ever will, or ever can, be forthcoming. The advancement of science is continually doing away with harsh, abrupt outlines, and revealing the softest shades of transition in the varied scenery of nature. Between organic and inorganic matter, between the inert and the living mass, the line of separation has been hitherto, to our minds, the hardest and sharpest of all. We have indeed become so accustomed to this violation of the cosmos, this harsh interruption to the continuous order of nature, and to the simplicity of its general plan, that we are apt to be rather annoyed than pleased with the first efforts made to prove them only imaginary. There is a dignity about life which requires, it is thought, to be defended from too close a proximity in character to the chemical solids and liquids amongst which it makes its appearance, even though the life whose dignity is thus maintained exhibit little more than the functions of a stomach, or be presented in the somewhat dull animation of a chrysalis and the torpor of a slug.

A *Wellingtonia gigantea*, with its stupendous height and graceful form, with its bark and wood, and sap and pith, and cones and innumerable spikelets, seems wonderfully noble and vastly superior in the scale of creation to a spoonful of salt; yet every one of the tiny grains has, so far as we know, full as much sense and as much power of enjoyment as the stately tree. The mineral and the vegetable are, in fact, alike destitute of any qualities on which a comparison of dignity can properly be founded. The organic depends ultimately upon the inorganic for its nutriment. It is itself ultimately reduced to the inorganic. It does not, therefore, seem incredible that living organisms, simpler perhaps than any yet detected by the microscope, should be or should have been produced without generation proper by the mere combining of inorganic materials.

This is the hypothesis of Spontaneous Generation, so called, or *abiogenesis*, unproved and extremely difficult of proof, but precisely filling that gap in the order and continuity of nature which is so puzzling without it.

Practically it makes no difference to the theory of development whether the simple organisms from which that theory supposes the more complicated to be derived, originated at a single era or at several. The theory does not deny the perpetuation throughout vast ages of extremely simple organisms. To the general cohesion of the theory, therefore, it is unimportant whether we affiliate each of these living motes to a parent like itself, or to a combination of chemical substances previously without life.

Considering the vast results attributed to the principle of *variability*, it has been thought strange that any organisms should through great cycles of time have escaped its operation, and transmitted their original simplicity to an endless succession of descendants.

On the hypothesis of spontaneous generation working continuously this difficulty would disappear; simple organisms would be continually losing their simplicity by variation, but new organisms of equal simplicity would continually appear in the world, spontaneously generated.

It might still be true that all but the least conspicuous members of the world's population belong to a single family, or to an extremely small number of separate lines of descent. If we suppose that, as soon as the globe was fitted for living occupants, a single simple organism was spontaneously generated, or, if you please, created, or, in any other way that may be named, introduced upon the earth, the results in accordance with actual facts may be logically deduced agreeably to the various principles of the theory of development. Its descendants would multiply and replenish the earth, unchecked, in all parts suited to their conditions of existence, till all such parts were occupied. No further advance in the population of the world could then take place until some variation had occurred, making possible the occupation of new regions, or of the old regions, under new conditions. But the new species, constituted by some advantageous variation, would be likely to overrun the whole field, to the almost complete suppression of the earlier and more simple form. The distance thus gained in the race of progressive organization it would be likely not only to maintain, but greatly to increase. Its descendants would vary in more than one useful direction, till it might, as we have said, become the parent of all the conspicuous members of the earth's population. The earliest and simplest form might still have representatives inheriting its likeness by direct descent, but unable to make their way in the world, not from wanting the power to vary, but from finding the world pre-occupied by species too powerful for them to compete with. In this way they would be restrained to their original insignificance.

Now exactly the same result would follow, if, instead of being born in what we consider the ordinary course of parentage, these simple forms were ever being spontaneously generated. They would find the world pre-occupied against their advancement in the scale of organization; they would rarely, if ever, be allowed to lead up by successive useful variations to highly-organized forms; and if ever, only in periods of time so enormous as to perplex the acutest human understanding.

What is commonly supposed to be the Biblical theory of Creation, is in truth a theory of spontaneous generation, only multiplying a million-fold the difficulty, if it be a difficulty, involved in that hypothesis. Unless we suppose the globe to have always existed, and always to have been tenanted by creatures endowed with life, we are forced to believe in the occurrence at some time or other of what, in the language of science, must have been spontaneous generation. As there is no historical reason for confining such an occurrence to any particular era; as science can give no reason why, if it happened once, it should not happen an indefinite number of times; as all analogy is in favour of uniform laws of nature rather than exceptional surprises; and, lastly, as numerous phenomena that have to do with the reproduction and maintenance of life are all continuous, and not interjectional—it seems at least an open question whether the origin of life itself may not also be sometimes, or even continually repeated. For, imagine what conditions we will to have prevailed when the elementary substances coalesced, out of which were compounded the first living being, it is difficult to imagine that the same conditions should never have recurred to produce a similar result, since the conditions are so far limited, that they must have been consistent, not only with the birth, but with the life after its birth, of that most antique animalcule. So many wonderful and hitherto unsuspected effects in the working of Nature have of late years been unveiled, so much of marvellous analysis successfully carried out, that it would surely be superstitious to despair of finding fresh links in the chain that binds together the lifeless and the living. Experiments in this direction may hitherto have failed from want of skill or care, or proper means at the command of those who conducted them. Yet it is not too much to ask of men renowned in science, that in pointing out the errors, they should abstain from discouraging the efforts.

Let it not be thought irreligious to anticipate the possible establishment of the supposition now under discussion. It cannot be irreverent to think that the bestowal of life upon a particle of matter too minute for human eye to see, requires no more special apparatus than that allotted to the exquisite crystals of the frost. ' Out of whose womb came the ice? and the hoary frost of heaven, who hath gendered it?' Yet in the workmanship of these a Divine hand is to the full as visible as in a diatom or a puff-ball. That the life-giving energy should have been exhausted in a single effort, is contrary beyond doubt to the analogy of religion, whatever may be thought of the analogy of nature.

On the other hand, let it not be thought unscientific to advocate the claims of an unproved hypothesis. It is the nature of hypotheses to be unproved. As they gather proof, the hypothetical becomes a theory. At length the theory goes on to demonstration. The use of hypotheses has often been explained. The human mind is easily exhausted by the observation of numerous incoherent facts. It is impelled to arrange and classify, to find some thread or threads of association on which the facts may be strung, some principle on which they may be parcelled out into groups. The arrangement may be erroneous, the explanatory principle untrue; they may be so plausible, so apparently satisfactory, so fascinating withal in general aspect, as for a long time to hinder the real solution of great problems; and nevertheless it may be judged that their services in the advancement of knowledge far outweigh the hindrances caused by the too servile acceptance accorded them. The foibles of a great writer may long infect the literature which his greatness has ennobled. A constitution grandly conceived in proportion to the moral and social ideas prevailing at the time of its conception may be clung to with servility long after it has been outstripped by the progress of civilization. But neither the genius of the poet nor the skill of the lawgiver could be spared in its own day and generation; neither could have been sacrificed to prevent the follies of the plagiarist, or the dulness of eyes that in after ages might read the letter without discerning the spirit.

We may almost say that a bad hypothesis is better than none; but a wrong hypothesis need not be a bad one. It may tend so to group around it the facts contributed by supporters and opponents, that when the real explanation of them all comes to be suggested, the fraternization of the confronting armies may be easy, and the truth be greeted and acknowledged with general acclaim.

THE IMPERFECTION

OF

THE GEOLOGICAL RECORD.

THE general who is for ever counter-marching and skilfully executing retrograde movements cannot always sustain the enthusiasm of his own troops, much less excite in his favour that of the civilian multitude. To many minds, the reliance placed on the imperfection of the geological record appears to be a rather damaging retreat in the strategy of science. They were just beginning to believe in geology as a wonderful revelation of the past history of the globe, when suddenly they are told that the fragments of that history which have been saved are merely tattered pages out of different chapters, giving no adequate notion of the enormous bulk and varied contents of the whole volume. Since, without the geological evidence of time's duration and of the countless changes in organic structures which that duration embraces, the theory of development could never have been imagined, it seems half ungrateful and inconsistent in the author of the theory to turn round upon geological evidence and tax it with its extreme poverty and even delusive misleading appearances. But, in fact, Mr. Darwin in no way detracts from the value of geological evidence. The researches necessary to extend it are invested, to those who accept his theory, with tenfold interest. The deficiencies and interruptions in it which he has pointed out as necessarily occurring must sooner or later have become apparent. They were dangerous to science only as long as they were unobserved, or not sufficiently taken into account.

That the record is really imperfect is not a matter which admits of controversy. No one supposes that every species and variety that ever existed in past ages on the globe is represented at this very day by fossil specimens in prime enough condition to exhibit all the characteristics of the creature as it once lived. No one supposes that, if such specimens existed, all of them ever could or would be found by human beings. It is not in the nature of a fossil to present all the characteristics of the creature as it once lived. It cannot possibly do it; for the fossil is without life and motion. There is no respiration, no circulation of the blood going on. As a rule, only the hard parts of the creature, such as shell, scales, or bony skeleton, can be preserved. In most cases all these relics have been chemically altered. Nevertheless, in fossils from the very lowest strata, from the very earliest formations that yield any, we find certain analogies to creatures now living. We reason from these analogies without any hesitation to the characteristics which the fossil creature will probably have presented in its living state. Our reasonings may often be erroneous, but the mere fact of our accepting the apparent analogies as a ground for reasoning at all, implies a belief in the uniformity of the conditions of animal existence between our own times and the most distant ages of the past. We argue as if generation had succeeded generation without interruption, not as if there had been new independent creations from time to time, since these would imply new conditions replacing the old, and make the argument from analogy between the items of the different creations of no value. For these independent creations, whether capricious or not in themselves, could only exhibit to our minds the symptoms of caprice. The mere fact of their being independent one of another would be so wanting in congruity with all the rest of our experience, that we should reasonably expect their minor details as well as the general plan to be wholly fantastic. In other words, the fossil memorials of life in past ages, imperfect as we confess and maintain them to be, still present so many general resemblances to one another and to living structures of the present day, that if they do not prove the continuity of life upon the globe, they cannot be held to prove anything at all; they should be regarded as a very elaborate practical joke played upon the human reason.

Palæontology is defined as 'the science which treats of fossil remains both animal and vegetable.' This principle of the continuity of life from age to age may be considered as one of its definite acquisitions. There is no single point of geological time at which it can be said, 'at this epoch clearly all old species had passed away, all kinds of life had become new.' Not only is there no indication of such a break, but there is the strongest evidence against any such having ever occurred. In spite, however, of the completeness of the evidence required for proving this single conclusion, the general incompleteness and enormous deficiencies in some parts of the palæontological record can be established beyond dispute. We are in the position of a man who has kept the title-deeds to a large estate, while almost all the estate itself has been buried under the encroachments of the sea. Here and there some old landmarks may be discernible far out in the waters, showing the extent of what had once been meadow and woodland, farm and garden, but unable to show how these were distributed, or to exhibit any of their details.

Mr. Parfitt, in his paper on 'Fossil Sponge Spicules,' told the Devonshire Association last year (1870) that we have evidence more or less exact of sponges in a fossil state as far back in time as the Silurian system, mentioning specimens of *Acanthospongia Siluriensis*, *Cliona antiqua*, and *Cliona prisca*, and stating in regard to the two latter that the genus is still in our own seas. He then referred to large masses of a fossil in the Devonian rocks of Cornwall, believed by some to be sponges, and by others to be the remains of fish. That these are in reality fish-remains has, in fact, been shown pretty conclusively[1]. From this point, however, up to the Great Oolite, Mr. Parfitt tells us that scarcely a vestige of the sponges is to be found, although since that time they have been very abundant. Between the Silurian and the Great Oolite the interval of time must have been enormous. It is occupied by a vast series of sedimentary rocks, embracing very varied mineral characteristics. From this series our museums have been, and are still being, supplied with vast heaps of fossil organic structures, including among numerous others, plants and corals and fish and reptiles. Through all that protracted period there is no reason to suppose, in regard to the outer rind of the globe, that the general conditions of earth, air, and water were other than they are now. All England may have been under water; delicate creatures may have wintered at the North Pole for the sake of its genial climate; and an infinity of other local and temporary differences may have prevailed, without making the habitable globe of those days essentially different from our own. The laws of chemistry and mechanics, the laws of heat and motion, must have been just the same as they are now. Then, as now, there must have been oceans and continents, winds and currents, forests growing, decaying, and being buried, sand and chalk being deposited in layers, molten minerals thrown up by volcanoes, ice forming at a

---

[1] See Mr. Pengelly's paper on the subject in the Transactions of the Devonshire Association for 1868.

definite temperature, glaciers scoring the rocks, icebergs transporting boulders, rains and rivers slowly washing down the hills, and waves corroding the cliffs on the sea-shore. We have evidence also that life in many forms abounded. Those forms, though seldom transmitted to creatures of the present day with anything approaching an exact likeness, can yet be classified under the same general names with the most modern forms of life. Now sponges are forms of an extremely simple organization. The silicious spicules are well adapted for the wear and tear of a fossil existence. In the greensand and the chalk they are actually found in extraordinary abundance. It would be inconvenient upon any theory to have to suppose these very simple structures introduced into the world for the first time quite late in the series of living organisms, and after beings much more complicated and higher in the scale of existence, unless, indeed, we suppose that about the time of the Great Oolite the evolution of man was first thought of, and the sponge accordingly prepared for him to wash his face with. But even if the bath and the basin be admitted as the final causes of sponge-existence, the conception of it must be carried back, as we have seen, to the Silurian period; while, according to Mr. Parfitt, the immense interval of Lias and Trias, Permian, Carboniferous, and Devonian remains black and spongeless, as though it were the appropriate era of the great unwashed. But if the Darwinian theory be a true one, sponge-life having begun in the Silurian period, and being in existence now, must have been continuous through the whole interval; every single deposit in the entire series since the Silurian must have been contemporary with some of the sponges; and, as a matter of fact, Mr. Parfitt's statement, however true of the condition of our knowledge a few years back, must now be qualified by the addition of several species spread over the interval in Britain alone, even if we exclude some indefinite structures, of which no opinion can be at present pronounced with safety. Mr. Parfitt himself, in a paper read at Honiton in 1868, remarks that 'the Devonian formation has furnished a great number of specimens of what appear to be species of sponges.' From Permian and Triassic beds on the continent of Europe, a very large number of forms are said to be more or less distinctly made out. Mr. Salter, in 1864, reported the discovery of Protospongia Fenestrata in the Lingula flags of St. David's, thus carrying back this form of life beyond the Silurian to the Cambrian era. It is an interesting illustration of the great ambiguity of these ancient fossils, that two such authorities as Mr. Salter and Dr. Bowerbank differed about the Protospongia, the one supposing it to exhibit the spicules, the other the fibre of the sponge. The simple facts that species have to be moved backwards and forwards between the amorphozoic and zoophytic groups, that relics may pass for fish in one year and sponges in another, and by-and-by be recognised again as fish, show the often imperfect condition of the record, even where it is not a complete blank.

Where direct evidence of any kind is still unavailable,

it may possibly be said that no sponges are found for such and such a period, because none existed in it. The plausibility of such an opinion can only be tested in fresh illustrations of the general argument. The coal-field of Nova Scotia has been described by Professor Dawson of Montreal. As it afforded a fine field for the exertions of the geologist, so it repaid him by its great richness in the fossil remains of plants. But in the coal formations of England and of Westphalia insects also had been found of different genera in addition to plants, while Nova Scotia, with all its vegetable wealth, yielded the anxious explorer but a single specimen of the still more interesting relics. That specimen consisted of the head and some other fragments of a large insect, probably neuropterous. That single specimen Professor Dawson tells us he found in a coprolite, in the fossil excrement of a reptile enclosed in the trunk of an erect sigillaria. Could any one invent a more curious cabinet to preserve so fragile a specimen for millions of years? Can it in this case be argued, that of insect remains nothing was found in the carboniferous of Nova Scotia but the head and some other appurtenances of a single neuropterous insect, because that head and those appurtenances were all that had ever flourished there? It cannot so be argued, not only because the analogies of the carboniferous formation in other parts of the world are conclusive against such argument, but also because within the last three or four years, after long and diligent search, two more species have been added to the collection of carboniferous insects from Nova

Scotia itself. Two delicate wings, one very large and one small, have been found, each sealed, as it were, with a fern-leaf; each a frail but enduring record of life that must once have been brilliant and abundant[1].

When the zeal of a collector adds a new species to those already known, by finding the fragment of a butterfly's wing that had been for millions of years in a seam of coal, how many considerations are forced upon the mind! Our sensitive nerves are comparatively seldom troubled by the perceived presence of dead creatures. With the exception of our own food, such sights are pretty well confined to the carcase of a dog floating on a pool, the feathers of a torn bird, a parched mole, and a sprinkling of blue-bottles in an unused room. Yet countless millions of creatures are annually dying, ready and willing to become fossils. Fossils, however, they do not become, simply because other creatures eat them up. For this reason alone, not one in ten thousand of any particular terrestrial species is likely to become fossil, because to some creature or another it is almost sure to be good eating, and therefore in the living state or the dead, sure to be ravenously seized upon and devoured.

Some forms of marine life are indeed represented by a wonderful number of specimens or fragments of specimens. Silicious and calcareous exuviæ of minute creatures deposited in the still depths of the ocean may be preserved by myriads, but neither these 'in number numberless' nor the giant-bones of ancient Saurians convey any adequate notion of the whole population of

---

[1] 'Acadian Geology,' Dawson, p. 386.

the globe at any one era. The palæontologist, guiding himself only by prominent details of this description, would be like a child over a child's history of England, to whom the fabric of the Constitution and the Reformation of the Church seem matters obscure, and scarcely worthy of notice, while Alfred burning the cakes, and Henry VIII in his well-known character of Bluebeard, stand out in bold relief.

No one will doubt, that within the last ten years tens of thousands of the common white butterfly have disported themselves in England, yet a man might easily starve if he were allowed no food till he had found some of their fossil remains. The dodo has not long been extinct, but nevertheless fossil dodos are extremely rare. It may be thought that the date of extinction has little to do with the matter, and that each relic when enshrined in the rock, may claim to be by a sort of indelible character 'once a fossil and always a fossil.' This, however, is in reality far from its true condition. Let a creature's remains escape being devoured, or burnt, or trampled to pieces, or being dissolved by the rain, or crumbled into dust by rolling waves and mud and stones gathered upon them, their perils are not yet over. Even in the grasp of the hard rock, the fossil may be horribly distorted by pressure, split asunder by cleavage, boiled and baked and crystallized, till none of its features remain what they were, or till the very fact of its presence becomes only the question of a dim surmise. The rude jolt of an earthquake, that splits asunder a mountain, may sometimes be tender over a butterfly's wing; but there are chemical agencies which work without any compassion for what is fine and delicate, and by these we find great thicknesses of rock apparently stripped of their fossils. Where the whole stratum consists of remains of once living organisms, as in seams of coal, it has been shown that we have no reason to suppose that any complete or adequate memorials are left us of the whole vegetation of any particular period or any particular area; since Dr. Lindley has found, by actual experiment, that different vegetables have very different powers of resisting decay, and that pines and ferns and lycopodia will be well preserved after long immersion in water, while the same treatment causes the disappearance of grasses and sedges, of the oak-tree and the ash[1].

Even those rocks which preserve fossils most carefully may themselves be crumbled to pieces, fossils and all, by the process of denudation.

Denudation is the laying bare of one stratum, or portion of a stratum, by the removal of another. It is carried on principally by rains and rivers and the action of the sea-waves upon the sea-border. To the last-mentioned agency the geologist is highly indebted; to the others also he owes a debt: but consider how they all do their work. Much of the material dealt with they pound into mud or sand, and in these any fragments that escape the trituration are, sooner or later, again buried. They may tear open the rocks, and expose for a brief period the most interesting and unique fossils;

[1] See 'Lecture on Coal,' by W. Boyd Dawkins, Esq., M.A., F.R.S. Manchester, 1870.

but, unfortunately, they carry on their work by night as well as day, on desolate coasts, in places where the Palæontographical Society has no missionaries, or when the missionary, if there be one, is in-doors writing a book; so that a very small percentage of all that might be discovered is ever actually found.

In the artificial denudation of mining and quarrying, though the rude forces of Nature are dispensed with, the enlightened hammer of the geologist can do very little by itself. In most cases it can but follow where commercial enterprise leads the way, and be grateful for permission to rummage among the *débris*, when pickaxe and blasting have done their work.

The chances against a fossil's being found to any useful purpose in quarrying are very numerous. The rock must chance to split so as to disclose it; the workman must chance to notice it; he must chance to have knowledge enough to think it worth notice; have time enough to stop from his work and take it; have sense enough to keep it safe; have memory enough to recollect where he hides it; and, lastly, have the luck to meet with a customer who knows its scientific value.

Numbers of rare specimens must continually be consigned to the furnace and the limekiln, or buried under mounds and hills of refuse. Sometimes the character of the matrix, by its hardness or its softness, makes it impossible to disengage the fossil without complete disfigurement; sometimes the fossil itself is so fragmentary as rather to confuse than to teach. Dr. Hooker gives an instance, in which a geologist assigned three pieces of fossil-leaf to plants of three different genera, which a subsequent observer maintained to be merely the separated portions of a single leaf of one and the same plant [1].

In the slates and limestones of Torquay, full as they are of marine fossils, no fish-remains have been identified, with one exception. Yet these rocks have been searched by numerous sharp eyes and clever hands, professional as well as amateur, with regular investigation, and in the sometimes more successful trifling of idle moments. It is worthy of note that the one exception is no scarcely decipherable relic, the nature of which might remain an open question, but a beautiful and finely-preserved scale of *phyllolepis concentricus* [2]. Had there been only one fish in the 'Devonian' waters of the neighbourhood, the one fish must have had more than one scale; yet none of the others are forthcoming. The science of to-morrow may find them; to the science of to-day they are lost irrecoverably.

The still-living varieties of the oyster are a miserable remnant of the 255 fossil species from the chalk described in Coquand's recent work. Professor Flower, in reviewing this monograph, remarks, that 'with these mollusks, numerous as they are, there are no forms that can fairly be recognized as transitional.' But inasmuch as the succession in time of these species is well-established by the different zones of the chalk in which they are found, we must either accept some nine or ten successive creations concerned in the production of oysters,

---

[1] Address to the British Association, 1868, p. 66 of the Report.
[2] In the Collection of W. Pengelly, Esq., F.R.S.

or we must allow the various fossil species to be connected with one another by descent. Upon the latter alternative, a whole chain of transitional links must once have existed between the earliest form of oyster and the latest; and though many of these links have been preserved, still more must have been lost, or deprived of their distinctive features; so that here, where the geological record is, to all appearance, unusually perfect, its actual imperfection is more clearly than ever established.

To conclude, then, in few words :—The majority of dead creatures never become fossils at all.

The majority of fossils perish miserably in their hiding-places.

Of those that are saved, the majority cannot be got at by man.

Of those that can be, the majority never are.

Of those that are, a large number prove illegible; a large number are fragments; a large number duplicates; and, lastly, a large number fall into hands which again lose or destroy them.

We cannot therefore argue, because fossils of such-and-such forms of life have never been found, that such-and-such forms never existed. They may have existed, and left no fossils. The fossils may have been left, and subsequently destroyed. The fossils may be undestroyed, but never have been found. The sum-total of acquisitions is small, but precious; it never can make a complete record, but it may make one sufficiently ample to establish the Darwinian Theory, or to replace it by some still wider and still simpler generalization.

DARWINISM.

THE NOACHIAN FLOOD.

Sir,—A friendly correspondent has done me the honour of noticing my lecture on the Noachian Flood in more than one contribution to your columns. The easy way in which he admits the possibility of a partial deluge and of pre-Adamite races, together with other symptoms of liberal thought and a trust in the conclusions of science, makes me tremble to think what would have befallen him had he lived 'in happier ages of the Church.' At the same time these dangerous and lamentable tendencies towards free-thinking make it needless for me to urge upon him those other and further conclusions towards which he is evidently of his own accord rapidly finding his way. But there are numerous persons who may read his pleasantly-written letters without perceiving how very far gone he himself is from the original simplicity of an unquestioning faith, and may, therefore, fancy that he is a champion of orthodoxy putting down an anti-Scriptural disputant, or showing at least, if he shows nothing more, that the questions in dispute are still too unsettled and vague for plain folks to meddle with or understand. Such a result is directly opposed to that which my lecture aimed at, which was to show plain folks that the subject not only could be understood, but ought to be; to convince them, if possible, that on this subject, and perhaps a few others, they were bound by all the laws of truth and honesty either to learn what there was to be learned, or for the future to hold their peace. Two striking examples were quoted, from the lives of Columbus and Galileo, to show that theologians had dragged the Holy Scriptures through the dirt, by presuming to use their authority for a purpose for which it was never designed, in a province to which it never lays claim, namely, the trial of evidence in natural science. It seems to have escaped the notice of your correspondent, that geography and astronomy were no more advanced in those days than geology and palæontology in our own. But will any one presume to tell us that the Bible is a match for struggling infant sciences, and may be quoted to contradict, suppress, and crush them, but that when they are full-grown it must in turn succumb to their dictation? That is indeed the principle on which, in the old Greek comedy, the son justifies his thrashing his aged father, because in bygone years, when their strength was different, his aged father had thrashed him. Only this, we must remember, is the invention of an incomparable satirist, meant for avoidance, not for imitation.

It may be remarked, by the way, that in taking objection to the opening sentence of the lecture, my friendly opponent seems to have misconceived its purport. 'Darwinism implies,' it says, 'almost throughout, that no universal deluge has drowned our globe, either within the last ten thousand years, or even within a period indefinitely longer.' Now, since certainly no Darwinian accepts the old views about the Deluge, this sentence could scarcely have been written for the benefit of Darwinians; and it would have been a very unsophisticated piece of rhetoric to say to a popular audience —'Darwinism is true, so you see the old views about the Deluge are false,' seeing that the popular audience might have disposed of the argument by the simple plan of interchanging the two adjectives. But the lecture opens with an acknowledgment that a recent universal deluge would be an argument sufficient to upset the Darwinian Theory, prior to showing that so important an objection to the theory is itself on numerous independent grounds untenable. Some arguments are equally in harmony with Darwinism, and inconsistent with the universality of the Noachian Flood. One of these is to be found in the existing diversities of the human race: but your correspondent appears to suppose that the element of time has nothing to do with the theory of development, when he says that 'to represent the divergence of races as impossible in any given period, however short, is strange ground for a Darwinian to take up.' He might as well require an engineer to believe that an engine had been driven at six hundred miles an hour, because the engineer himself believed it to have been driven at the rate of fifty or sixty. He only half states the argument against a common Noachian descent founded on the difference between the

Papuans and the Malays. The striking point is, that these two contrasted races are separated by almost the very same line which separates two great zoological provinces. On the old supposition of migration from the ark, that the lower animals, as well as men, should have 'agreed to differ' on the opposite sides of a narrow deep-sea channel, was indeed a remarkable bundle of coincidences.

That traditions of a deluge are wide-spread is acknowledged. That they are traditions of a universal deluge neither is nor can be proved. That with all their local variations and discrepancies they point to one and the same deluge, is a question of probability, much more proper to follow than to lead the main argument. We shall not gain much for science or religion out of the story of Deucalion's flood, which attributes the origin of the new stock of men and women to the pebbles that Deucalion and his wife threw over their shoulders; an ancestry surely less dignified even than that from the orang-outang and the gorilla with which Mr. Pengelly and Professor Huxley are supposed to have mortified the dignity of mankind.

It is surprising that so many good Christian people should feel touchy on this question of an enormously remote ancestry, although they would, upon occasion, join with earnestness and true humility in the confession that 'dust we are, and unto dust shall we return.' In their reluctance even to examine the real truth of the question, they fail to perceive that the true sons of the Prophets are not their lineal descendants, but those who inherit their wisdom; and that 'a man's a man for a' that,' although his great-grandfather should prove to have been a lob-worm or a toad-stool.

Too much injury to religion has been done already by confounding false science with Scriptural truth, to make it either 'fair or reverent' to hold back from protesting, whenever occasion offers, against the mischief. Persons accustomed with presumptuous or careless ignorance to denounce geology and Darwinism, and the results connected with them, may have had their consciences soothed and encouraged by your correspondent. My charitable object is to make those consciences uneasy again[1].

March 23rd, 1870.

[1] This and the three following letters were originally addressed to the Editor of the *Torquay Directory*, in answer to a gentleman who, in company with large multitudes of his fellow-Britons, both male and female, holds and upon occasion upholds a mass of opinions on Science and Religion, any one of which opinions individually may be right or may be wrong, but which, when held collectively, seem to my humble understanding to be logically incoherent.

SCIENCE AND RELIGION.

Sir,—One of your correspondents has pithily observed, that if he has denounced Darwinism, it is simply because he believes it to be untrue. Could you not, Sir, in the interests of science and Christian charity, prevail upon him to recal his denunciation, by showing him that intellectual error requires not to be denounced, but to be set right? The prejudice against Darwinism has undoubtedly arisen from a conflict—real or apparent—between its conclusions and certain passages of Scripture. Such a prejudice arose against the earlier advancement of astronomy and geology, and the new conclusions arrived at were 'denounced in the interests of Christian orthodoxy,' *simply because those who denounced them believed them to be untrue.* It is a little sad, though withal a little amusing, to observe how many persons, eminent at once for piety and Protestantism, inveigh against the Papal assumption of infallibility, while assuming an infallibility of their own. They know precisely what is Scripture doctrine and what is not. They know exactly what measure of inspiration God has been pleased to give to this writer or the other. At one time they are sure that a science is not true, because the Bible does not speak in accordance with the language of the science; at another time they discover that the science had all along been very clearly revealed in the Bible under a disguise. It unfortunately escapes their notice that by this means, while they are reverently denouncing the science 'in the interests of Christian orthodoxy,' they are under a disguise denouncing the Bible.

'In my view,' says your correspondent above referred to, 'the Mosaic writers were divinely taught, and knew what they wrote about with a most perfect knowledge.' In one sense, no doubt, they *did* know what they were writing about — they knew that it was religion, and, therefore, they never pretended to 'enunciate' science, whether false or true; but in any other sense to say that they knew what they wrote about with a most perfect knowledge, is to assert what is highly improbable, and cannot be proved. Either it makes every writer a kind of god, so far as the attribute of infallibility is concerned, or it destroys all independence of testimony. To claim for them a perfect knowledge of which they made no use, except to mislead the world for thousands of years, is surely to commit the capital offence of 'inciting to hatred and contempt' of their writings. How alien, moreover, is it to the spirit of the writers themselves — men who are constantly confessing their own errors, doubts, and perplexities; men whose path in moral, let alone intellectual excellence, was not always direct and straightforward, and who knew and owned their infirmity of nature. How contrary, too, to every analogy of life is this notion of a Book, written in perfect language by men of perfect knowledge in every subject that may be even incidentally referred to in its pages. For not only is man an imperfect being, but his language is an imperfect instrument of his imperfect thoughts. His conscience is fallible; his understanding is fallible; let the Book which guides him be as infallible as you please, he will still bring it back to the inherent imperfection of things human by misreading and misconceiving it. That the law of God is perfect, follows from the very thought of God; that any particular exposition of that law to finite minds either is or can be perfect, is almost, or altogether, a contradiction in terms. Far from knowing all about modern systems of Botany, Moses did not even know all about religion as the later prophets knew; nor did *they* know as we know. Their mission would probably have been hidden rather than forwarded, had they been able to 'enunciate' scientific truths in advance of their age. Their new views in religion were often roundly abused; their new views in science would hardly have escaped denouncing.

As a caution to the unwary, it should be remarked that the opposition supposed to exist between Mr. Darwin's phrase 'Natural Selection,' and Mr. Herbert Spencer's 'Survival of the Fittest,' is purely imaginary. The latter, no doubt, is the more philosophically accurate, the former is a convenient, popular, and telling metaphor. They both express the same conception of a large and wonderful group of facts. Perhaps it will be scarcely necessary to caution the unwary against taking for granted that 'vestigiform structures are proofs of a typical formation;' but if they are, they prove that in the typical formation of man a tail was included, which would be such a disgrace to the typical formation as would prevent all worthy and decorously-minded persons from believing in typical formations for a moment.

DARWINISM, AND THE FIRST VERTEBRATE.

Sir,—Your amiable and earnest correspondent does not seem to understand that men like Darwin and Wallace, who have spent years of patient labour and thought in amassing observations of nature, and grouping together the facts out of which their theories have been formed, have a right to 'an air of philosophical superiority,' if they choose to display it, when questions are asked or arguments put forward which imply ignorance or misconception of all they have been doing in the interests of science. When Mr. Wallace 'very coolly' asserts that he sees no force in an argument, it will as a rule be advisable for the argument either to withdraw itself from the public gaze, or get itself stated a little more lucidly. Again, when Mr. Darwin 'rashly affirms that he has distinct evidence' of a thing, it would perhaps be a good plan to get the Commissioners in Lunacy to examine the astonishing number of hard-headed men whom he induces to believe his unfounded assertion.

But now that I have prevailed with your correspondent to give up 'denouncing' Darwinism, I wish further to press upon him the advantage of ceasing to 'deny' it, and, above all, of ceasing to deny it with any admixture of religious phraseology in his denial. He has himself allowed that sciences, seemingly most at variance with the language of Scripture, have come to be reconciled with it; he must see, therefore, that the appearances of Scriptural language can be no objection to Darwinism or to any other scientific theory whatever. Darwinism is founded on the comparison of an enormous number of well-ascertained facts issuing in a few generalizations of extreme importance if true, but also of considerable importance, even if far short of the truth. Every hypothesis which will explain a large number of hitherto disconnected facts, though it may be in itself erroneous, helps and guides men in the end towards the true explanation. To 'deny,' or, in other words, to make a public protest against such hypotheses without having anything better or equal, or a tenth part as good to offer in their stead, is to be a hinderer of science, and, instead of being really pious and reverent, is a very pretty, though doubtless unconscious imitation of that rhetoric which, because of the acknowledged difficulties in every form of religion, 'denies' religion altogether.

That your correspondent *does* lay just a little tiny claim to infallibility is clear from the very letter in which he modestly disowns it: for he therein prays always to be enabled to think and act about the interpretation of Scripture as he now thinks and acts, which would be a foolish prayer, if his present thoughts and actions might possibly be wrong or misguided. And yet he differs from a very large number of divines, in supposing that the prophets, for instance, knew all that their own prophecies portended; so that if all those worthy divines be right in assuming that the inspired writers did not always 'know what they wrote about,' then your correspondent, who makes the contrary supposition, must be wrong,—and there will still be some hope for Darwinism.

It is scarcely fair to ask for space to answer his momentous challenge about the first vertebrate, or to explain the thoroughly sceptical form which the challenge assumes. When the Apostle Thomas said, 'except I see the print of the nails, I will not believe,' he had no logical claim to receive the proof of the resurrection which he demanded, because *a priori* it would have been quite fair to suppose our Lord's resurrection-body would retain no such signs of previous outrage; and it is a kindred mistake to suppose that the truth of the development-theory in any way hinges upon the possibility of constructing an effigy of the first vertebrate either as it actually was, or to suit an anti-Darwinian's notions of what it ought to have been. According to the development-theory, it must have been the product of innumerable antecedent factors, itself the heir of many far-descended and often modified characters; and yet, for all that, it will probably have been a far simpler organism than the simplest modern vertebrate. It is well known by what insensible gradations the natural kingdoms and the classes in those great divisions pass, so to speak, into one another; it need, therefore, cause no surprise if the primary vertebrate of all the vertebrates should prove neither to have been fish, flesh, fowl, nor good red herring; but for an actual specimen of a living vertebrate that can neither 'swim, crawl, fly, nor walk,' I cannot do better than refer my philosophical opponent to a new-born baby.

THE FIRST VERTEBRATE, AND THE BEGINNING OF REASON.

Sir,—Against your correspondent's preference for vernacular terms may be set a remark by Dr. Whewell, that 'the loose and *infantine* grasp of common language cannot hold objects steadily enough for scientific examination, or lift them from one stage of generalization to another. They must be secured by the rigid mechanism of a scientific phraseology.' To say that 'the first vertebrate must have been the product of innumerable antecedent factors,' is, perhaps, an expression more puzzling than if one merely said that 'its immediate progenitors' were 'a single pair;' but then it has the advantage of being considerably more suggestive, and a good deal more to the purpose. Among these 'factors' of a living creature parents commonly find a place,—two parents generally; in some cases, only one; in some cases, not even one, if we are to believe the advocates of spontaneous generation, or the still popular view in regard to the Creation. To the parental factors of any particular offspring must be added those which are constituted by food and climate and a multitude of changes and chances in the whole course of its existence. Some characters it may derive from remote ancestors, transmitted through, though not developed in, its 'immediate progenitors.' It is now forty years since two French anatomists showed the possibility, or even probability, of a connection between the molluscous cuttle-fish and the vertebrate type; and, considering the propensity of the highest vertebrate for perpetually squirting ink at those who meddle with it, most readers of controversy will think the instance well selected. Those who wish to be told what the first vertebrate was probably like, should first accurately define what they mean by a vertebrate. Is a jointed backbone the only essential? And if so, how many vertebræ are essentially requisite? A creature with two vertebræ would be as much a vertebrate as a creature with three. What shall we say, then, of a creature possessing, if we may use the expression, but a single vertebra? It would not have a jointed backbone. It would not be a vertebrate. Yet, by the simple multiplication of similar parts, in accordance with a thousand analogies, a vertebrate could be developed from it. By the differentiation of these similar parts, which not only might follow, but must follow, a great variety of species could easily be evolved. Those who really take an interest in the problems connected with this subject, and whose 'convictions' are not too strong and absolute to be swayed by ascertained facts and logical reasoning will do well to study the 'Principles of Biology,'

Herbert Spencer. They will there see by what extraordinarily simple gradations the lowliest organisms are connected with higher and the highest forms. They will there find that 'modification of characters' is a doctrine less intricate than might be supposed, even if it cannot be wholly explained in words of one syllable.

If any intelligent persons can discern the undulatory theory of light and the modern system of botany in the first chapter of Genesis, no one would wish to complain of their ingenuity, unless they proposed to support a particular theory of inspiration by these discoveries. But then, if the theories of science are only 'the undulations of human opinion,' it becomes necessary to ask why the botanical undulation of the present day is accepted as a witness, and the Darwinian undulation rejected. Had the famous Pagan critic, to whom your correspondent 'R. T. E.' refers, imagined the sentence, 'Let there be light, and there was light,' to be a scientific description instead of a theological one, we may feel sure that he would have condemned it for bombast instead of praising it for its majesty of expression. As it is, he does not declare it to be the sublimest sentence ever uttered, but remarks that 'the lawgiver of the Jews, no common man, having comprehended the power of the divinity according to the just conception of it, unfolded it agreeably thereto,' both in this and in the parallel phrase, 'Let the dry land appear, and it was so.' That all things which *are* and which *become,* both are what they are and become what they become by the simple fiat of the supreme God, is a piece of elementary philosophy and religion, which, I conceive, Sir, none of your correspondents can have any wish to dispute; but that the writer of Genesis anticipated by his scientific knowledge the epoch of Copernicus and Newton, Young and Fresnel, Linnæus, De Jussieu and Cuvier, is not only not proven by the few simple phrases of his writings that have anything remotely to do with the branches of science which they so nobly illustrated; much more than this, it would be a disgrace and heavy imputation upon him had he known all *they* believed, and yet expressed himself so badly as to leave the world for thousands of years in ignorance of the very germs of the true theories, so obscurely that no one should ever have dreamed that he was alluding to the true theories till after they had been independently discovered.

Your correspondent 'X^n' will find both his pleasure and his profit in reading the chapter on Instinct in 'Darwin's Origin of Species.' It will give him some idea, I say not, how the reasoning faculty was first acquired, but how it may have been gradually developed. By a careful study of the same work he, and many others who need the knowledge, will see that in accordance with Darwinism the deterioration of a species is quite possible. His quaintly expressed argument about Adam's 'immediate progenitor' omits to notice that in the moral world it is a step upward to become capable of sinning, just as in the physical world it is a step upward to become capable of dying, so that the wretchedest man with reason is higher in the scale than the noblest dog, and the humblest plant than the costliest and most beautiful stone. The other difficulty which he puts forward of an abrupt transition between the first man with reason and the parents of such a man without reason is a difficulty, like that in regard to the first vertebrate, one of words rather than of facts. As with the origin of language and of languages, as with the origin of the natural kingdoms and of every individual form of life, so with the origin of reason; could we see the whole series of steps, with their infinitely numerous and sometimes almost infinitely fine and subtle points of discrimination, we should probably be unable to fix upon any one definite division and say, here noise ends and articulate language begins; or, here Saxon ends and English begins; or, *this* is the top of instinct, and *this* the dawn of reason.

OYSTERS OF THE CHALK,

AND THE THEORY OF DEVELOPMENT[1].

THE interesting notice in your last number, of M. Coquand's 'Oysters of the Chalk,' draws inferences unfavourable to the theory of development or evolution which scarcely seem warranted by the facts. It need not be 'difficult to imagine the creature as existing under such conditions, that one species, while engaged in "the struggle for existence," should starve out and extinguish another;' for however widely we may find a fossil species dispersed, it is not probable that it occupied the whole of its territory at one and the same time, and in the limited area occupied immediately before its extinction, new varieties may have prevailed over and displaced the old by some slightly superior adaptation to the food-supply of the region. The extinction of any particular species may in some instances have been due to the extinction, or loss by other means, of its own appropriate food. Again, it is not necessary to suppose that the hinge, or the internal or external structure of the shell of an oyster, has been altered by

[1] Reprinted from 'Nature,' No. 30.

what may be called the direct action of 'natural selection,' since by the well-established principle of 'correlation' the variation in one part of an organism is nearly or quite certain to produce variations in other parts. 'If any such change did occur,' it is argued, 'it must have been *per saltum*, since with these mollusks, numerous as they are, there are no forms that can fairly be recognised as transitional.' But this appeal to the evidence of facts is somewhat premature. The immense difference pointed out between the geological records of England and France in regard to these very oysters of the chalk, leaves it perfectly open for us to suppose that even the comparatively full French record is itself exceedingly imperfect, and that the transitional forms have either not been preserved, or remain yet to be discovered. Mr. Darwin gives reasons for believing that when variation once begins it continues with some vigour; hence, between two settled wide-spread species connected genealogically together we might expect a large number of transitional varieties, each represented by only a few individuals, so that the whole number of these transitional forms might well be lost to the genealogical record.

Finally, the objection from the scarcity of oysters at the present day, compared with the great abundance of species in the past, does not really touch the theory of development, which is concerned to explain how species come into existence, not how they go out of it. That varieties, species, genera, have been superseded or extinguished, within longer or shorter periods, is a fact admitted on all hands. The general principle of natural selection will account for this in the rough, maintaining as it does that fresh varieties, species, and genera better adapted to the surrounding circumstances have arisen, and by their superior adaptation unavoidably ousted the older forms. Digging down into the records of history we find a time when the Romans were supreme in the civilized world; no two consecutive years of the interval present any remarkable divergence of the prevailing conditions, yet now we may say of that Roman supremacy in the civilized world, that, 'like the Mastodon, it is a thing of the past.'

Torquay, May 14, 1870.

THE MATHEMATICAL TEST

OF

NATURAL SELECTION[1].

THE soul of many an anti-Darwinian will have been cheered by Mr. A. W. Bennett's paper on 'The Theory of Natural Selection from a Mathematical Point of View.' It is, in fact, a very admirable piece of special pleading, based on a skilful assumption of premises which, to a careless or biassed observer, might seem indisputable.

The tendency to variation is spoken of as something very mysterious, of which no adequate account has ever yet been given. Yet the very simple explanation is no bad one,—that where two parents are concerned in the production of any offspring, the product in part resembling each of the producers must of necessity also in part differ from each of them. Between the parents themselves, Mr. Herbert Spencer has shown that differences of age and external circumstances would ensure the requisite want of resemblance in the absence of any other cause.

'The rigid test of mathematical calculation' is then

[1] Reprinted from 'Nature,' No. 56.

applied to the case of mimetic butterflies, with the view of showing that they could not have been produced simply according to the laws of variation, inheritance, and natural selection. In the application of this rigid test, the very first step is a perfectly gratuitous assumption, 'that it would require, at the very lowest calculation, one thousand steps to enable the normal *Leptalis* to put on its protective form.' Who is to prove that fifty differences would be insufficient? An interval of a thousand years might be granted for establishing each one of these variations. Suppose even fifty thousand, instead of only fifty steps, to be necessary, it is another gratuitous assumption that 'the smallest change in the direction of the *Ithomia*, which we can conceive on any hypothesis to be beneficial to the *Leptalis*, is at the very lowest one-fiftieth of the change required to produce perfect resemblance.' How small a difference must decide the choice made by a donkey placed equidistant between two bundles of hay! Certainly, then, a bird on the wing, having to choose amidst myriads of butterflies, may be determined by an almost infinitesimal distinction. Further, though the whole change may be produced by an immense number of small changes, it is not necessary to suppose that all the changes will be equally small. It is merely begging the question to assume that the first change could not possibly be large enough to be of any use. And if it may be of use, the whole mathematical calculation, based on its being useless, breaks down from the beginning. Again, since the *Leptalis* may have spent one million years in arriving at its present likeness to the present *Ithomia*, it is impossible to assert that the normal forms of the two butterflies were as wide apart at the beginning of that period as they are at present. The mimicry having once set in, might be retained by parallel variations. This, indeed, cannot fail to be the case, if the protection is to be a lasting one; for when the *Ithomia* varies in outward appearance, unless the *Leptalis* varies in the same direction, the resemblance will be lost. This progressive mimicry would be more valuable than an imitation in which no changes occurred, since the enemies of a mimetic species would in time become aware of a fraud which had no variations at its command, as birds are said now-a-days to pounce without hesitation upon caterpillars which very much resemble twigs[1]. Even 'a rough imitation' may be useful in the first instance, and yet when hostile eyes have long been exercised, and have acquired greater and greater sharpness, finally nothing less than *absolute identity* of appearance may be thoroughly effective. Thus the perfecting of the resemblance will be no 'mere freak of Nature,' nor shall we be 'landed in the dilemma that the *last* stages are comparatively useless' in this procedure.

The array of figures brought forward to prove that the *Leptalis* could not have made twenty steps of variation in the direction of the *Ithomia by chance*, would be much to the purpose if any exponent of the theory of Natural

---

[1] Applying to these caterpillars Mr. A Murray's recent hypothesis for explaining 'mimicry' by hybridization, we should draw the poetical inference that a happy marriage is possible between a butterfly and a rose-bush.

Selection had ever argued or supposed that it could. The calculation takes it for granted that the theory is erroneous, instead of proving it to be in error. Upon this assumption, it might have been put far more strongly, only that a stronger way of putting it would have borne on the face of it the suspicion of some inherent fallacy. It begins by supposing that there are 'twenty different ways in which a *Leptalis* may vary, only one of these being in the direction ultimately required;' it might quite as truthfully, or even more so, have said a thousand instead of twenty, and then the second step would have given the chance as only one in a million, instead of one in four hundred. But while the theory of Natural Selection speaks of numerous minute useful variations, Mr. Bennett will not allow that combination of terms. Let them be numerous and minute, if you will, he says; but if small, they cannot be useful; if useful, they cannot be small. He claims to have Mr. Darwin's own word for it, that a large variation would not be permanent, as though Mr. Darwin had said, 'living creatures have come to be what they are by successive useful deviations of structure permanently propagated, but no large deviations are permanent, and no small ones are useful.' It is quite obvious that in the use of relative terms, such as great and small, Mr. Darwin neither intended to stultify himself nor has done so. A thing may be large enough to be useful without being large as compared with something twenty times its own size; and a man may be said to have a huge brain in a very small body, although the body in solid content far exceeds the brain. When Mr. Darwin says that 'Natural Selection always acts with extreme slowness, he does not imply that its steps must therefore be so numerous as to be too small to confer any advantage. This would be a contradiction in terms. But the steps may be exceedingly small notwithstanding, and also sometimes separated by enormous intervals of time from one another.

In introducing his own explanation of things, Mr. Bennett affirms that ' resemblances, and resemblances of the most wonderful and perfect kind' in the vegetable kingdom, ' are in no sense mimetic or protective.' This may be so, but it can hardly be said to be proved. When he speaks of 'man's reason' having ' assisted him so to modify his body as to adapt himself to the circumstances with which he is surrounded,' and suggests that the instinct of animals may have assisted them also to modify their bodies by slow and gradual degrees to the same purpose, it is difficult to imagine the process intended, and still more difficult to see how ' the slow and gradual degrees' will escape the rigid test of mathematical calculation which Mr. Bennett has elsewhere applied; for if the steps are great, they ought not to be permanent; and if small, they ought not to be useful. A theory which makes it possible for a bee to 'modify its proboscis' by instinct, or for a man to treat his nose in the same manner by reason, seems harder of digestion than the Darwinian.

Torquay, Nov. 12, 1870.

THE GENESIS OF SPECIES.

A review in 'Nature,' by Mr. A. W. Bennett, of Mr. Mivart's 'Genesis of Species,' contains the following passage :—

'It behoves, therefore, every Darwinian to satisfy himself that either Mr. Mivart's premises or his line of argument is unsound.

'The objections brought forward by the author are summed up as follows :—(1) That Natural Selection is incompetent to account for the incipient stages of useful structures. (2) That it does not harmonize with the co-existence of closely similar structures of diverse origin. (3) That there are grounds for thinking that specific differences may be developed suddenly instead of gradually. (4) That the opinion that species have definite though different limits to their variability is still tenable. (5) That certain fossil transitional forms are absent which might have been expected to be present. (6) That some facts of geological distribution supplement other difficulties. (7) That the objection drawn from the physiological difference between "species" and "races" still exists unrefuted. (8) That there are many remarkable phenomena in organic forms upon which Natural Selection throws no light whatever, but the explanations of which, if they could be attained, might throw light upon specific origination.

'If these objections are not new, they are at least sustained by new arguments. They are evidently of very unequal value. The third is very difficult of proof or disproof. The fifth may be true in our present state of knowledge, but would be very unsafe by itself as the basis of an argument. The first, second, and eighth are of greatest value, and are those which Mr. Mivart has most closely worked out[1].'

The review containing the above passage did not appear till the present volume was on the very eve of publication. Even a hasty glance at Mr. Mivart's book is sufficient to show that Mr. Bennett has not over-estimated its importance and value. It is scarcely possible here to do more than make a few reflections upon its general scope, in reply to the challenge offered to Darwinians. The first objection, as it stands in the summary, wears the appearance of a misconception. It is almost certain to produce one. When Mr. Darwin attributes the origin of species to Natural Selection, he includes expressly, and where not expressly, by obvious implication, the principle of Variability. He never maintains that the first or any subsequent stage of a useful structure can be produced by Natural Selection. Natural Selection only operates to preserve. Without Variation it would have no sphere in which to operate, so that

[1] 'Nature,' No. 65.

from one point of view Mr. Darwin may be said to attribute the origin of species to Variation rather than Natural Selection. He is, moreover, far from ignoring the influence of other principles, such as Inheritance, Reversion, and Correlation, upon the total result. He may be thought inconsistent with himself in laying stress at times upon the minuteness of the variations which he supposes to have slowly accumulated into specific differences, and at other times admitting the sudden appearance of variations which may be considered as large ones, and which are certainly striking. But in the first instance the great and almost overwhelming difficulty was to induce a belief that forms specifically different could be connected with one another by descent. By showing that a multitude of small differences accumulated would make a large total difference, he made as it were a bridge for the existing incredulity. It now appears that the gulf may be passed with easy strides instead of the little slow steps at first thought necessary. This fortifies the doctrine of the Transmutation of Species, in proportion as there are fewer 'missing links,' fewer transitional forms that need to be accounted for.

Of 'the coexistence of closely similar structures of diverse origin,' illustrated so forcibly by the instance of the eye, 'in at least three independent lines of descent, the Mollusca, the Annulosa, and the Vertebrata,' it can scarcely be denied that Natural Selection alone would be an inadequate explanation. But here again it should be observed that Darwinism does not attribute everything to Natural Selection. It assumes, what must be allowed, that variations occur. In obedience to what laws those variations themselves are produced is an interesting speculation, and a most important subject of inquiry. That such laws or conditions of Variation exist no one can doubt, unless he has been seduced by Ovidian metamorphoses to believe in trees bleeding human blood and human foreheads branching with the antlers of the stag. A knowledge of those conditions might fully explain the coexistence of similar structures of diverse origin, consistently with the principle of Natural Selection. The ignorance of them is scarcely a proof that such coexistence does not harmonize with it.

The objection that giraffes, which profited by long necks in a time of drought, would find them a disadvantage subsequently, as requiring a greatly increased size and strength of muscles to support them, overlooks the law of correlation, by assuming that the elongated neck would be out of proportion to the other conditions of the creature's fabric.

Mr. Mivart's fourth objection seems at least an extremely improbable opinion. He refers to Mr. Darwin's expression, that the goose appears to have a highly inflexible organization, as if he himself thought it possible for a species at length to attain to an organization completely inflexible. Such a view would imply two parents exactly like one another, producing offspring exactly like themselves; and of such exact likenesses no known families afford examples.

The seventh objection recalls the still unexplained physiological difference between 'species' and 'races,' unions between the former being sterile, and between the latter fertile. In this branch of the subject there is much scope still for inquiry. Some of the difficulty may be due to a trick played us by language. True species have been defined to be those that are not fertile together; and from the definition it follows that races which *are* fertile together are not true species. But the question is obscured by the use of the two different words 'races' and 'species,' the real issue being, whether races that are and races that are not fertile together can originate in the same way. The subject in its other bearings has been largely discussed by Mr. Darwin in his work on 'Animals and Plants under Domestication.'

It remains only to say a few words on the argument from the calculation of chances which is supposed to reduce the survival by natural selection of any particular useful variation almost or altogether to an arithmetical impossibility. 'The advantage,' we are told, 'whatever it may be, is utterly outbalanced by numerical inferiority. A million creatures are born: ten thousand survive to produce offspring. One of the million has twice as good a chance as any other of surviving: but the chances are fifty to one against the gifted individual's being one of the hundred survivors. No doubt the chances are twice as great against any one other individual, but this does not prevent their being enormously in favour of *some* average individual[1].' In this calculation it seems to be overlooked that every individual will vary more or less, and that out of a million variations there is a very great probability that *one* should give much more than the amount of advantage which the calculation supposes. Nor does it follow that a variation conferring great advantage in the struggle for life should be great in comparison with a creature's general organization. There is a very probable alternative, that when the advantages are exceedingly slight they may be shared by a great many, and that when falling to the lot of only one or a few, they may be exceedingly important. The doctrines of reversion and inheritance are pressed into the service of the arithmetical argument to show that the acquired advantage would be gradually diminished and finally lost. But Mr. Darwin tells us that, 'when a new character appears, it is occasionally from the first well-fixed[2].' The chances upon one principle that a character will not be transmitted are not worth consideration, if, under the operation of some other principle known or unknown, the transmission of the character actually takes place. We are asked whether one white man, introduced into an island otherwise inhabited only by negroes, would be likely to give the whole island eventually a white, or even a yellow, population. Without trying the experiment, we may perhaps safely answer in the negative. But

---

[1] 'Genesis of Species,' p. 57, quotation (somewhat obscure as it stands) from the North British Review for June, 1867.

[2] 'Animals and Plants under Domestication,' vol. ii. p. 63.

the illustration loses much or all of its point, when we consider how little the circumstances of the experiment would correspond with what ordinarily happens in nature, how little we know whether the white man's colour would be really an advantage or the reverse, and how complicated are the differences between a white man and a negro. If the blackness of the negro be due to Natural Selection in any considerable degree, we should expect it to suit the conditions which surround him in his native habitation better than a white skin would do. In this case the pallor introduced into the breed by a solitary stranger would gradually disappear in obedience to the principles of Natural Selection, not in opposition to them. To take once more the instance of the giraffe; the useful variation is here by hypothesis an elongated neck; it is conceivable that out of large herds the few survivors of a drought might be exclusively such as possessed this advantage to some extent. These would probably transmit to a large majority of their descendants the tendency to vary in a given direction which they had themselves all more or less exhibited. Their progeny, moreover, would be placed in exceptionally favourable circumstances by the very fact that in the previous drought so many of the same species had been starved to death, who would otherwise have furnished their chief competitors in the struggle for existence. It is still objected that upon this supposition many other animals ought to have acquired giraffe-like necks. But such an expectation is far from being warranted by the principles of Natural Selection.

Since all variations are potentially useful, but only those are preserved which suit the surrounding conditions among which they are exhibited, the calculation of chances will itself plead for the probability that a variety of variations will be preserved, rather than the same many times over. Other species competing with the giraffe for food would be little likely to gain an advantage over it by a slight increase in length of neck, though by other variations they might achieve a decided superiority. It is obvious, also, that the advantage assigned to the elongated neck would belong to many other possible variations, such as a lengthened proboscis, far-reaching arms, the climbing powers of the snake or the monkey, the flight of the bird or the insect; all of which may be due to Natural Selection and the subsidiary principles which the theory of Development embraces.

The calling in of subsidiary principles may be thought to spoil the boasted simplicity of the theory. But such an opinion is hypercritical. One might truthfully say of a great patriot that all he did was in obedience to the simple law of duty, without implying that he was exempt from the law of association of ideas, or independent of the mechanical, chemical, and vital laws which regulate many of the functions of all human beings alike.

INDEX.

Abiogenesis, note on hypothesis of, 126–132.
Addison, his opinion about Instinct, 71; his description of the brood-hen, 72; his account of a hen with brood of ducks, 73; on the insensible gradations of species, 74.
African desert, geological evidence of, 122.
Anabas scandens, its climbing powers, 28; Dr. Day's opinion thereon, 28, note.
Androcles, story of, 82.
Animal mounds, of Wisconsin, 105.
Ants, slave-making, 29, 69; French philosopher's account of, 73.
Artificial selection, part of Natural selection, 16.

Baboons, warfare of, 69.
Bacon, Lord, his statement about dogs, 75.
Barbarism, time required for development of, 57.
Bees, progress of, in cell-making, 25; their accuracy over-rated, 69, 86.
Bennett, Mr. A. W., Mathematical test applied by, 168; Review by, 173.
Birds' nests, reasoning powers employed in construction of, 69, 86; compared with human dwellings, 70; use of human manufactures in, 71.
British Association, exploration of Kent's cavern by, 109.

Britons, ancient, condition of, 111.
Brookes, Henry, story of a lion quoted from, 76.
Brutes, man's treatment of, 11, 90; opinion that God is the soul of, 71; compared with men, 74; their moral qualities, 75, 88; their laws and constitutions, 77; their perceptions and emotions, 80; language of scripture about, 84; motives of pleasure and pain applied to, 88; children compared with, 89.

Cannibalism, 57; of British tribes, 112.
Caterpillars, resembling twigs, 170.
Chalk, continuous formation of, 117.
Civilization, its dependence on language and the art of writing, 88.
Coal-measures, 119–121, 140.
Columbus, his opinion of the earth's spherical form condemned, 60, 148.
Coquand's Oysters of the Chalk, Professor Flower's review of, 145, 165.
Correlation, 17, 166, 176.
Creation, sudden, not reconcilable with the order of nature, 25; theories of, compared, 32; prejudice in favour of its suddenness, 63, 64; Biblical theory of, 129.
Creations, many distinct, not warranted by scripture or science, 20, 116, 135; special, for special localities, untenable, 21.

Danes, ancient, food and weapons of, 104.
Darwin, his account of the development of his theory, 4; his calculation about elephants, 13; allusion to his theory of Pangenesis, 33; his explanation of the fauna and flora of mountain-tops, 46; his account of slave-making ants, 69; his treatment of geology, 134, his chapter on instinct, 163.
Darwinism, 3-33; obscurely anticipated, 2; its supporters, 3; prejudice against, 4, 152; its bearing on the seeming imperfection of nature, 24; inconsistent with a recent universal deluge, 31, 34.
Dawkins, Mr. W. Boyd, lecture on coal by, 143.
Dawson, Dr., Acadian Geology, 120, 140.
Day, Dr., paper by, on the Mud-fish and Anabas scandens, 28.
Denudation, 143.
Deucalion's Flood, argument from rebutted, 150.
Development, theory of, by whom originated and supported, 4; opinion of its absurdity, 6; facts and principles necessary to, (variation, 7; Inheritance and Reversion, 9; struggle for life, 11; antiquity of the globe, 30; freedom of the globe from any recent universal catastrophe 31); application of, to human body and mind, 62, 95; time required for, 122; not materially affected by hypothesis of spontaneous generation, 127.
Ducklings, experiment with, 73.

Earth, immense age of, required by Theory of Development, 30, 67; proved by geology, 31, 54, 107, 121; popular impression as to age of, 93, 121; reckoned by millions of years, 123.
Egypt, its monuments, 51; its chronology, 56, 101.
Elephant, its sagacity, 3; its rate of breeding, 13; its different species, 46; its memory, 66; epithet applied to it by Pope, 74; in Devonshire, 112.
Esquimaux, their ignorance of arithmetic, 103.

Flint-tools, 109, 111, 113.
Flood, the Noachian, 34-61; historical account of, 38; explanation suggested, 41; how consistent with Darwinism, 50; traditions of a, 58; no traces of its universality, 59.
Food, its influence on the animal and vegetable kingdoms, 12; in the competition for life, 22.
Fossils, an evidence of variation, 20; different in different strata, 116; time required for vicissitudes of, 119; necessary imperfection of, 134; their scarcity and abundance, 141; numerous chances of loss and destruction for, 146.
Fuegians, nakedness of, 112, *note*.

Galileo, his doctrine of the earth's motion condemned, 60, 148.
Genesis, book of, its chronology, 55.
'Genesis of Species,' by Mr. Mivart, 173.
Geology, its conclusions, 31, 53; imperfection of its record, 133-146.
Giraffes, 176, 179.
Glacial Period, its effect on distribution of species, 47.
Gooseberry, the big, 16.

Horse, career of, in America, 48; its endurance and ambition, 3; its intelligence, 66; instance thereof, 74; its intercourse with man, 80.
Hypotheses, use of, 131.

Inheritance, 9; at different periods of life, 18.
Instinct, of bees, 25; employment and gradations of, in various animals, 28; compared with reason 62-81, 164; fallacious theory of, 67; ignored by ducklings, 73; fancied excellence of, 86.

Kent's cavern, 109-115.

INDEX.

Language, time required for variations of, 57; its influence on mankind, 77, 87; origin of, 103.
Light, rapidity of, 97.
Limestone, formation of, 109; contents of, 115; slow formation of, 117; Devonian, older than the New Red Sandstone, 118.
Lindley, Dr., his experiment with immersed vegetables, 143.
Linnæus, on the common descent of species, 3.
Lion, its generosity, 3; instance of its affection, 76; instance of its gratitude, 83; in Britain, 112.
Locke, on the reason of brutes, 74.
Lubbock, Sir John, 'Pre-historic Times,' 54, 104, 107, 112; 'Origin of Civilization,' 107.
Lyell, Sir Charles, 'Principles of Geology,' 3, 54; 'Antiquity of Man,' 107; 'Elements of Geology,' 109.

Madagascar, its species and genera, 46.
Malay, compared with the Papuan by Mr. Wallace, 49, 150.
Man, his destructiveness, 11; his likeness to other animals in blood, fibre, and skeleton, 29; distribution of his varieties, 48; traced back for thousands of years, 51; a common origin for all families of, 52; his chief endowments, 67; compared as a builder with birds, 70; his brain and hairless skin, 73; his bodily structure, 85; his opinion of war, 86; real origin of, forgotten, 102.
Marriage-customs, slow change of, 106.
Marsupials, 46; fossil, 47.
Matlock Bath, formation of stalagmite at, 110, 114.
Memory, necessary to intelligence, 66; unequal distribution of, 66.
Miracles, treatment of false ones, 40; of the Old Testament, 83.
Mivart, St. George, Mr., 'Genesis of Species' by, 173.

Mushroom, time required for its growth, 55.
Mygale, the trap-door spider, its ingenious nest, 29.
Natural Selection, illustrated by artificial selection, 14; the slowness of its movement, 18; explains the order of nature, and in part its seeming disorder, 26; limits of, propounded by Mr. Wallace, 62.
Nile, articles in sediment of, 108.

Origin of life, opinions on, 94.
Oysters, memory of, 66; obscure politics of, 77.

Palæontology, Lyell's definition of, 135.
Papuan, compared with the Malay, 49, 150.
Parfitt, Mr., on Fossil Sponge Spicules, 136, 139.
Pengelly, Mr., on pre-historic man, 105; exploration of Kent's cavern by, 109, 110, 113.
Pigeons, subjected to man's selection, 14, 16, 17.
Plants, their struggle for food, 12; their movements, 28.
Pope, his epithet for the elephant, 74.

Reason, progressive development of, in individual minds, 62, 67; that of men, one in kind with the intelligence of brutes, 66, 84; helps to, 86.
Relative terms, 97, 171.
Religion, development of, 64, 90.
Reversion, 9; limits artificial selection, 17.
Rudimentary organs, 21.

Sandstone, New Red, 118.
Savages, question of their degeneracy, 57; brain, skin, and voice of, 78.
Science, not antagonistic to Christian doctrine, 82, *note*.
Scripture, no warrant for distinct creations, 20; does not profess to

teach Natural Science, 35; its use of ordinary language, 36; its historical account of the Flood, 38; explanation thereof, 41; disregard of secondary causes in, 83; character of genealogies in, 99; mistaken quotation of, 124; invidious connection of, with false science, 151; supposed opposition between it and Darwinism, 157.

Species, permanence of, 9; some benefited by change of habitat, 21; variations of, how advantageous, 27; difficulty of collecting all for the Ark, 43; distribution of, 45.

Spencer, Mr. Herbert, his caution about embryonic forms, 19, *note*; his accurate phrase, 'Survival of the fittest,' 154; his 'Principles of Biology,' 161.

Sponges, not to be hurried, 117; range of in geology, 136; final cause of, 138.

Stalagmite, thickness of in Kent's cavern, 110; time required for forming, 113; dates carved upon, 115.

Stratification, uniform order of, 116, 122.

Struggle for life, 11; great fecundity useful to a species in, 24.

Sylvia Sutoria, the tailor-bird, its nest, 29.

Tails, rudimentary, in man, 22, 155.
Tennyson, language of 'the Brook' in, 125.
Theories, when to be accepted, 18.
Thought, time required for, 64; movement of, depending on language, 87.

Time, immense duration of, required by the Theory of Natural Selection, 30, 67; lapse of, 93-125; (see *Earth*, age of); inexhaustible, 98, 125.
Tinière, delta of, 107.
Tyndal, Professor, on 'The Minuteness of Waves of Light,' 97.

Usher, archbishop, Bible-chronology of, 99, 110.

Variability, 7; objection to, considered, 128.
Vertebrate, the first, how originated, 158; type of, supposed to be connected with cuttle-fish, 161; definition of, investigated, 161.
Vivian, Mr., exploration of Kent's cavern by, 109.

Wallace, Mr., his originality recognized, 5; his opinion of the limits of Natural Selection, 62; his exposure of fallacious views about Instinct, 67; his theory of birds' nests, 69; his comparison of birds with men as builders, 70; his speculation about the brain of the savage, 78.
War, in the animal and vegetable kingdoms, 12; combination of baboons for, 69; comparison of man and other animals engaged in, 86.
Wasps, their defensive weapon, 25; materials used by, 86.
Whewell, Dr., his remark on Scientific Phraseology, 160.
Writing, invention of, 103.

[JANUARY 1871.]

GENERAL LIST OF WORKS

PUBLISHED BY

Messrs. LONGMANS, GREEN, AND CO.

PATERNOSTER ROW, LONDON.

History, Politics, Historical Memoirs, &c.

The HISTORY of ENGLAND from the Fall of Wolsey to the Defeat of the Spanish Armada. By JAMES ANTHONY FROUDE, M.A. late Fellow of Exeter College, Oxford.
    LIBRARY EDITION, 12 VOLS. 8vo. price £8 18s.
    CABINET EDITION, in 12 vols. crown 8vo. price 72s. each.

The HISTORY of ENGLAND from the Accession of James II. By Lord MACAULAY.
    LIBRARY EDITION, 5 vols. 8vo. £4.
    CABINET EDITION, 8 vols. post 8vo. 48s.
    PEOPLE'S EDITION, 4 vols. crown 8vo. 16s.

LORD MACAULAY'S WORKS. Complete and Uniform Library Edition. Edited by his Sister, Lady TREVELYAN. 8 vols. 8vo. with Portrait, price £5 5s. cloth, or £8 8s. bound in tree-calf by Rivière.

An ESSAY on the HISTORY of the ENGLISH GOVERNMENT and Constitution, from the Reign of Henry VII. to the Present Time. By JOHN EARL RUSSELL. Fourth Edition, revised. Crown 8vo. 6s.

SELECTIONS from SPEECHES of EARL RUSSELL, 1817 to 1841, and from Despatches, 1859 to 1865; with Introductions. 2 vols. 8vo. 28s.

VARIETIES of VICE-REGAL LIFE. By Sir WILLIAM DENISON, K.C.B. late Governor-General of the Australian Colonies, and Governor of Madras. With Two Maps. 2 vols. 8vo. 28s.

On PARLIAMENTARY GOVERNMENT in ENGLAND: Its Origin, Development, and Practical Operation. By ALPHEUS TODD, Librarian of the Legislative Assembly of Canada. 2 vols. 8vo. price £1 17s.

A HISTORICAL ACCOUNT of the NEUTRALITY of GREAT BRITAIN DURING the AMERICAN CIVIL WAR. By MOUNTAGUE BERNARD, M.A. Chichele Professor of International Law and Diplomacy in the University of Oxford. Royal 8vo. 16s.

The CONSTITUTIONAL HISTORY of ENGLAND, since the Accession of George III. 1760—1860. By Sir THOMAS ERSKINE MAY, C.B. Second Edition. 2 vols. 8vo. 33s.

A

The **HISTORY of ENGLAND**, from the Earliest Times to the Year 1866. By C. D. YONGE, Regius Professor of Modern History in the Queen's University, Belfast. New Edition. Crown 8vo. price 7s. 6d.

The **OXFORD REFORMERS of 1498**—John Colet, Erasmus, and Thomas More; being a History of their Fellow-work. By FREDERIC SEEBOHM. Second Edition, enlarged. 8vo. 14s.

A **HISTORY of WALES**, derived from Authentic Sources. By JANE WILLIAMS, Ysgafell. 8vo. 14s.

LECTURES on the HISTORY of ENGLAND, from the earliest Times to the Death of King Edward II. By WILLIAM LONGMAN. With Maps and Illustrations. 8vo. 15s.

The **HISTORY of the LIFE and TIMES of EDWARD the THIRD**. By WILLIAM LONGMAN. With 9 Maps, 8 Plates, and 16 Woodcuts. 2 vols. 8vo. 28s.

The **OVERTHROW of the GERMANIC CONFEDERATION by PRUSSIA** in 1866. By Sir ALEXANDER MALET, Bart. K.C.B. With 5 Maps. 8vo. 18s.

The **MILITARY RESOURCES of PRUSSIA and FRANCE**, and RECENT CHANGES in the ART of WAR. By Lieut.-Col. CHESNEY, R.E. and HENRY REEVE, D.C.L. Crown 8vo. price 7s. 6d.

WATERLOO LECTURES: a Study of the Campaign of 1815. By Colonel CHARLES C. CHESNEY, R.E. late Professor of Military Art and History in the Staff College. New Edition. 8vo. with Map, 10s. 6d.

STAFF COLLEGE ESSAYS. By Lieutenant EVELYN BARING, Royal Artillery. 8vo. with 2 Maps, 8s. 6d.

DEMOCRACY in AMERICA. By ALEXIS DE TOCQUEVILLE. Translated by HENRY REEVE. 2 vols. 8vo. 21s.

HISTORY of the REFORMATION in EUROPE in the Time of Calvin. By J. H. MERLE D'AUBIGNÉ, D.D. VOLS. I. and II. 8vo. 28s. VOL. III. 12s. VOL. IV. 16s. VOL. V. price 16s.

CHAPTERS from FRENCH HISTORY; St. Louis, Joan of Arc, Henri IV. with Sketches of the Intermediate Periods. By J. H. GURNEY, M.A. New Edition. Fcp. 8vo. 6s. 6d.

MEMOIR of POPE SIXTUS the FIFTH. By Baron HUBNER. Translated from the Original in French, with the Author's sanction, by HUBERT E. H. JERNINGHAM. 2 vols. 8vo. [*Nearly ready.*

IGNATIUS LOYOLA and the EARLY JESUITS. By STEWART ROSE. New Edition, preparing for publication.

The **HISTORY of GREECE.** By C. THIRLWALL, D.D. Lord Bishop of St. David's. 8 vols. fcp. 8vo. price 28s.

GREEK HISTORY from Themistocles to Alexander, in a Series of Lives from Plutarch. Revised and arranged by A. H. CLOUGH. New Edition. Fcp. with 44 Woodcuts, 6s.

CRITICAL HISTORY of the LANGUAGE and LITERATURE of Ancient Greece. By WILLIAM MURE, of Caldwell. 5 vols. 8vo. £3 9s.

The **TALE of the GREAT PERSIAN WAR**, from the Histories of Herodotus. By GEORGE W. COX, M.A. New Edition. Fcp. 3s. 6d.

HISTORY of the LITERATURE of ANCIENT GREECE. By Professor K. O. MÜLLER. Translated by the Right Hon. Sir GEORGE CORNEWALL LEWIS, Bart. and by J. W. DONALDSON, D.D. 3 vols. 8vo. 21s.

HISTORY of the CITY of ROME from its Foundation to the Sixteenth Century of the Christian Era. By THOMAS H. DYER, LL.D. 8vo. with 2 Maps, 15s.

The HISTORY of ROME. By WILLIAM IHNE. English Edition, translated and revised by the Author. Vols. I. and II. 8vo. [*Just ready.*

HISTORY of the ROMANS under the EMPIRE. By the Very Rev. C. MERIVALE, D.C.L. Dean of Ely. 8 vols. post 8vo. 48s.

The FALL of the ROMAN REPUBLIC; a Short History of the Last Century of the Commonwealth. By the same Author. 12mo. 7s. 6d.

A STUDENT'S MANUAL of the HISTORY of INDIA, from the Earliest Period to the Present. By Colonel MEADOWS TAYLOR, M.R.A.S. M.R.I.A. Crown 8vo. with Maps, 7s. 6d.

The HISTORY of INDIA, from the Earliest Period to the close of Lord Dalhousie's Administration. By JOHN CLARK MARSHMAN. 3 vols. crown 8vo. 22s. 6d.

INDIAN POLITY: a View of the System of Administration in India. By Lieutenant-Colonel GEORGE CHESNEY, Fellow of the University of Calcutta. New Edition, revised; with Map. 8vo. price 21s.

HOME POLITICS; being a consideration of the Causes of the Growth of Trade in relation to Labour, Pauperism, and Emigration. By DANIEL GRANT. 8vo. 7s.

REALITIES of IRISH LIFE. By W. STEUART TRENCH, Land Agent in Ireland to the Marquess of Lansdowne, the Marquess of Bath, and Lord Digby. Fifth Edition. Crown 8vo. price 6s.

The STUDENT'S MANUAL of the HISTORY of IRELAND. By MARY F. CUSACK, Author of the 'Illustrated History of Ireland, from the Earliest Period to the Year of Catholic Emancipation.' Crown 8vo. price 6s.

CRITICAL and HISTORICAL ESSAYS contributed to the *Edinburgh Review*. By the Right Hon. LORD MACAULAY.
CABINET EDITION, 4 vols. post 8vo. 24s. LIBRARY EDITION, 3 vols. 8vo. 36s.
PEOPLE'S EDITION, 2 vols. crown 8vo. 8s. STUDENT'S EDITION, 1 vol. cr. 8vo. 6s.

HISTORY of EUROPEAN MORALS, from Augustus to Charlemagne. By W. E. H. LECKY, M.A. Second Edition. 2 vols. 8vo. price 28s.

HISTORY of the RISE and INFLUENCE of the SPIRIT of RATIONALISM in EUROPE. By W. E. H. LECKY, M.A. Cabinet Edition, being the Fourth. 2 vols. crown 8vo. price 16s.

GOD in HISTORY; or, the Progress of Man's Faith in the Moral Order of the World. By Baron BUNSEN. Translated by SUSANNA WINKWORTH; with a Preface by Dean STANLEY. 3 vols. 8vo. price 42s.

The HISTORY of PHILOSOPHY, from Thales to Comte. By GEORGE HENRY LEWES. Third Edition. 2 vols. 8vo. 30s.

The MYTHOLOGY of the ARYAN NATIONS. By GEORGE W. COX, M.A. late Scholar of Trinity College, Oxford, Joint-Editor, with the late Professor Brande, of the Fourth Edition of 'The Dictionary of Science, Literature, and Art,' Author of 'Tales of Ancient Greece,' &c. 2 vols. 8vo. 28s.

HISTORY of CIVILISATION in England and France, Spain and Scotland. By HENRY THOMAS BUCKLE. New Edition of the entire Work, with a complete INDEX. 3 vols. crown 8vo. 24s.

HISTORY of the CHRISTIAN CHURCH, from the Ascension of Christ to the Conversion of Constantine. By E. BURTON, D.D. late Prof. of Divinity in the Univ. of Oxford. Eighth Edition. Fcp. 3s. 6d.

SKETCH of the HISTORY of the CHURCH of ENGLAND to the Revolution of 1688. By the Right Rev. T. V. SHORT, D.D. Lord Bishop of St. Asaph. Eighth Edition. Crown 8vo. 7s. 6d.

HISTORY of the EARLY CHURCH, from the First Preaching of the Gospel to the Council of Nicæa. A.D. 325. By ELIZABETH M. SEWELL, Author of 'Amy Herbert.' New Edition, with Questions. Fcp. 4s. 6d.

The ENGLISH REFORMATION. By F. C. MASSINGBERD, M.A. Chancellor of Lincoln and Rector of South Ormsby. Fourth Edition, revised. Fcp. 8vo. 7s. 6d.

MAUNDER'S HISTORICAL TREASURY; comprising a General Introductory Outline of Universal History, and a series of Separate Histories. Latest Edition, revised and brought down to the Present Time by the Rev. GEORGE WILLIAM COX, M.A. Fcp. 6s. cloth, or 9s. 6d. calf.

HISTORICAL and CHRONOLOGICAL ENCYCLOPÆDIA; comprising Chronological Notices of all the Great Events of Universal History: Treaties, Alliances, Wars, Battles, &c.; Incidents in the Lives of Eminent Men and their Works, Scientific and Geographical Discoveries, Mechanical Inventions, and Social, Domestic, and Economical Improvements. By B. B. WOODWARD, B.A. and W. L. R. CATES. 1 vol. 8vo. [*In the press.*

Biographical Works.

The LIFE of ISAMBARD KINGDOM BRUNEL, Civil Engineer. By ISAMBARD BRUNEL, B.C.L. of Lincoln's Inn; Chancellor of the Diocese of Ely. With Portrait, Plates, and Woodcuts. 8vo. 21s.

The LIFE and LETTERS of FARADAY. By Dr. BENCE JONES, Secretary of the Royal Institution. Second Edition, thoroughly revised. 2 vols. 8vo. with Portrait, and Eight Engravings on Wood, price 28s.

FARADAY as a DISCOVERER. By JOHN TYNDALL, LL.D. F.R.S. Professor of Natural Philosophy in the Royal Institution. New and Cheaper Edition, with Two Portraits. Fcp. 8vo. 3s. 6d.

The LIFE and LETTERS of the Rev. SYDNEY SMITH. Edited by his Daughter, Lady HOLLAND, and Mrs. AUSTIN. New Edition, complete in One Volume. Crown 8vo. price 6s.

SOME MEMORIALS of R. D. HAMPDEN, Bishop of Hereford. Edited by his Daughter, HENRIETTA HAMPDEN. With Portrait. 1 vol. 8vo. [*Just ready.*

A MEMOIR of G. E. L. COTTON, D.D. late Lord Bishop of Calcutta; with Selections from his Journals and Letters. Edited by Mrs. COTTON. With Portrait. 1 vol. 8vo. [*Just ready.*

The LIFE and TRAVELS of GEORGE WHITEFIELD, M.A. of Pembroke College, Oxford, Chaplain to the Countess of Huntingdon. By J. P. GLEDSTONE. 1 vol. post 8vo. [*Just ready.*

LIVES of the LORD CHANCELLORS and KEEPERS of the GREAT SEAL of IRELAND, from the Earliest Times to the Reign of Queen Victoria. By J. R. O'FLANAGAN, M.R.I.A. Barrister-at-Law. 2 vols. 8vo. 36s.

DICTIONARY of GENERAL BIOGRAPHY; containing Concise Memoirs and Notices of the most Eminent Persons of all Countries, from the Earliest Ages to the Present Time. Edited by W. L. R. CATES. 8vo. 21s.

LIVES of the TUDOR PRINCESSES, including Lady Jane Grey and her Sisters. By AGNES STRICKLAND, Author of 'Lives of the Queens of England.' Post 8vo. with Portrait, &c. 12s. 6d.

LIVES of the QUEENS of ENGLAND. By AGNES STRICKLAND. Library Edition, newly revised; with Portraits of every Queen, Autographs, and Vignettes. 8 vols. post 8vo. 7s. 6d. each.

MEMOIRS of BARON BUNSEN. Drawn chiefly from Family Papers by his Widow, FRANCES Baroness BUNSEN. Second Edition, abridged; with 2 Portraits and 4 Woodcuts. 2 vols. post 8vo. 21s.

The LETTERS of the Right Hon. Sir GEORGE CORNEWALL LEWIS, Bart. to various Friends. Edited by his Brother, the Rev. Canon Sir G. F. LEWIS, Bart. 8vo. with Portrait, price 14s.

LIFE of the DUKE of WELLINGTON. By the Rev. G. R. GLEIG, M.A. Popular Edition, carefully revised; with copious Additions. Crown 8vo. with Portrait, 5s.

HISTORY of MY RELIGIOUS OPINIONS. By J. H. NEWMAN, D.D. Being the Substance of Apologia pro Vitâ Suâ. Post 8vo. 6s.

The PONTIFICATE of PIUS the NINTH; being the Third Edition of 'Rome and its Ruler,' continued to the latest moment and greatly enlarged. By J. F. MAGUIRE, M.P. Post 8vo. with Portrait, 12s. 6d.

FATHER MATHEW: a Biography. By JOHN FRANCIS MAGUIRE, M.P. for Cork. Popular Edition, with Portrait. Crown 8vo. 3s. 6d.

FELIX MENDELSSOHN'S LETTERS from *Italy and Switzerland*, and *Letters from* 1833 *to* 1847, translated by Lady WALLACE. New Edition, with Portrait. 2 vols. crown 8vo. 5s. each.

MEMOIRS of SIR HENRY HAVELOCK, K.C.B. By JOHN CLARK MARSHMAN. Cabinet Edition, with Portrait. Crown 8vo. price 3s. 6d.

VICISSITUDES of FAMILIES. By Sir J. BERNARD BURKE, C.B. Ulster King of Arms. New Edition, remodelled and enlarged. 2 vols. crown 8vo. 21s.

THE EARLS of GRANARD: a Memoir of the Noble Family of Forbes. Written by Admiral the Hon. JOHN FORBES, and edited by GEORGE ARTHUR HASTINGS, present Earl of Granard, K.P. 8vo. 10s.

ESSAYS in ECCLESIASTICAL BIOGRAPHY. By the Right Hon. Sir J. STEPHEN, LL.D. Cabinet Edition, being the Fifth. Crown 8vo. 7s. 6d.

MAUNDER'S BIOGRAPHICAL TREASURY. Thirteenth Edition, reconstructed, thoroughly revised, and in great part rewritten; with about 1,000 additional Memoirs and Notices, by W. L. R. CATES. Fcp. 6s.

LETTERS and LIFE of FRANCIS BACON, including all his Occasional Works. Collected and edited, with a Commentary, by J. SPEDDING, Trin. Coll. Cantab. VOLS. I. and II. 8vo. 24s. VOLS. III. and IV. 24s. VOL. V. price 12s.

Criticism, Philosophy, Polity, &c.

The INSTITUTES of JUSTINIAN; with English Introduction, Translation, and Notes. By T. C. SANDARS, M.A. Barrister, late Fellow of Oriel Coll. Oxon. New Edition. 8vo. 15s.

SOCRATES and the SOCRATIC SCHOOLS. Translated from the German of Dr. E. ZELLER, with the Author's approval, by the Rev. OSWALD J. REICHEL, B.C.L. and M.A. Crown 8vo. 8s. 6d.

The STOICS, EPICUREANS, and SCEPTICS. Translated from the German of Dr. E. ZELLER, with the Author's approval, by OSWALD J. REICHEL, B.C.L. and M.A. Crown 8vo. price 14s.

The ETHICS of ARISTOTLE, illustrated with Essays and Notes. By Sir A. GRANT, Bart. M.A. LL.D. Second Edition, revised and completed. 2 vols. 8vo. price 28s.

The NICOMACHEAN ETHICS of ARISTOTLE newly translated into English. By R. WILLIAMS, B.A. Fellow and late Lecturer of Merton College, and sometime Student of Christ Church, Oxford. 8vo. 12s.

ELEMENTS of LOGIC. By R. WHATELY, D.D. late Archbishop of Dublin. New Edition. 8vo. 10s. 6d. crown 8vo. 4s. 6d.

Elements of Rhetoric. By the same Author. New Edition. 8vo. 10s. 6d. crown 8vo. 4s. 6d.

English Synonymes. By E. JANE WHATELY. Edited by Archbishop WHATELY. 5th Edition. Fcp. 3s.

BACON'S ESSAYS with ANNOTATIONS. By R. WHATELY, D.D. late Archbishop of Dublin. Sixth Edition. 8vo. 10s. 6d.

LORD BACON'S WORKS, collected and edited by J. SPEDDING, M.A. R. L. ELLIS, M.A. and D. D. HEATH. New and Cheaper Edition. 7 vols. 8vo. price £3 13s. 6d.

The SUBJECTION of WOMEN. By JOHN STUART MILL. New Edition. Post 8vo. 5s.

On REPRESENTATIVE GOVERNMENT. By JOHN STUART MILL. Third Edition. 8vo. 9s. Crown 8vo. 2s.

On LIBERTY. By JOHN STUART MILL. Fourth Edition. Post 8vo. 7s. 6d. Crown 8vo. 1s. 4d.

Principles of Political Economy. By the same Author. Sixth Edition. 2 vols. 8vo. 30s. Or in 1 vol. crown 8vo. 5s.

A System of Logic, Ratiocinative and Inductive. By the same Author. Seventh Edition. Two vols. 8vo. 25s.

ANALYSIS of Mr. MILL'S SYSTEM of LOGIC. By W. STEBBING, M.A. Fellow of Worcester College, Oxford. New Edition. 12mo. 3s. 6d.

UTILITARIANISM. By JOHN STUART MILL. Third Edition. 8vo. 5s.

DISSERTATIONS and DISCUSSIONS, POLITICAL, PHILOSOPHICAL, and HISTORICAL. By JOHN STUART MILL. Second Edition, revised. 3 vols. 8vo. 36s.

EXAMINATION of Sir W. HAMILTON'S PHILOSOPHY, and of the Principal Philosophical Questions discussed in his Writings. By JOHN STUART MILL. Third Edition. 8vo. 16s.

An OUTLINE of the NECESSARY LAWS of THOUGHT: a Treatise on Pure and Applied Logic. By the Most Rev. WILLIAM, Lord Archbishop of York, D.D. F.R.S. Ninth Thousand. Crown 8vo. 5s. 6d.

The ELEMENTS of POLITICAL ECONOMY. By HENRY DUNNING MACLEOD, M.A. Barrister-at-Law. 8vo. 16s.

A Dictionary of Political Economy; Biographical, Bibliographical, Historical, and Practical. By the same Author. VOL. I. royal 8vo. 30s.

The ELECTION of REPRESENTATIVES, Parliamentary and Municipal; a Treatise. By THOMAS HARE, Barrister-at-Law. Third Edition, with Additions. Crown 8vo. 6s.

SPEECHES of the RIGHT HON. LORD MACAULAY, corrected by Himself. People's Edition, crown 8vo. 3s. 6d.

Lord Macaulay's Speeches on Parliamentary Reform in 1831 and 1832. 16mo. 1s.

INAUGURAL ADDRESS delivered to the University of St. Andrews. By JOHN STUART MILL. 8vo. 5s. People's Edition, crown 8vo. 1s.

A DICTIONARY of the ENGLISH LANGUAGE. By R. G. LATHAM, M.A. M.D. F.R.S. Founded on the Dictionary of Dr. SAMUEL JOHNSON, as edited by the Rev. H. J. TODD, with numerous Emendations and Additions. In Four Volumes, 4to. price £7.

THESAURUS of ENGLISH WORDS and PHRASES, classified and arranged so as to facilitate the Expression of Ideas, and assist in Literary Composition. By P. M. ROGET, M.D. New Edition. Crown 8vo. 10s. 6d.

LECTURES on the SCIENCE of LANGUAGE, delivered at the Royal Institution. By MAX MÜLLER, M.A. &c. Foreign Member of the French Institute. 2 vols. 8vo. price 30s.

CHAPTERS on LANGUAGE. By FREDERIC W. FARRAR, F.R.S. late Fellow of Trin. Coll. Cambridge. Crown 8vo. 8s. 6d.

WORD-GOSSIP; a Series of Familiar Essays on Words and their Peculiarities. By the Rev. W. L. BLACKLEY, M.A. Fcp. 8vo. 5s.

A BOOK ABOUT WORDS. By G. F. GRAHAM, Author of 'English, or the Art of Composition,' &c. Fcp. 8vo. price 3s. 6d.

The DEBATER; a Series of Complete Debates, Outlines of Debates, and Questions for Discussion. By F. ROWTON. Fcp. 6s.

MANUAL of ENGLISH LITERATURE, Historical and Critical. By THOMAS ARNOLD, M.A. Second Edition. Crown 8vo. price 7s. 6d.

SOUTHEY'S DOCTOR, complete in One Volume. Edited by the Rev. J. W. WARTER, B.D. Square crown 8vo. 12s. 6d.

HISTORICAL and CRITICAL COMMENTARY on the OLD TESTAMENT; with a New Translation. By M. M. KALISCH, Ph.D. VOL. I. *Genesis*, 8vo. 18s. or adapted for the General Reader, 12s. VOL. II. *Exodus*, 15s. or adapted for the General Reader, 12s. VOL. III. *Leviticus*, PART I. 15s. or adapted for the General Reader, 8s.

A **HEBREW GRAMMAR,** with **EXERCISES.** By M. M. KALISCH, Ph.D. PART I. *Outlines with Exercises,* 8vo. 12s. 6d. KEY, 5s. PART II. *Exceptional Forms and Constructions,* 12s. 6d.

A **LATIN-ENGLISH DICTIONARY.** By J. T. WHITE, D.D. of Corpus Christi College, and J. E. RIDDLE, M.A. of St. Edmund Hall, Oxford. Third Edition, revised. 2 vols. 4to. pp. 2,128, price 42s. cloth.

White's College Latin-English Dictionary (Intermediate Size), abridged for the use of University Students from the Parent Work (as above). Medium 8vo. pp. 1,048, price 18s. cloth.

White's Junior Student's Complete Latin-English and English-Latin Dictionary. New Edition. Square 12mo. pp. 1,058, price 12s.

Separately { The ENGLISH-LATIN DICTIONARY, price 5s. 6d.
{ The LATIN-ENGLISH DICTIONARY, price 7s. 6d.

An **ENGLISH-GREEK LEXICON,** containing all the Greek Words used by Writers of good authority. By C. D. YONGE, B.A. New Edition. 4to. 21s.

Mr. **YONGE'S NEW LEXICON,** English and Greek, abridged from his larger work (as above). Revised Edition. Square 12mo. 8s. 6d.

A **GREEK-ENGLISH LEXICON.** Compiled by H. G. LIDDELL, D.D. Dean of Christ Church, and R. SCOTT, D.D. Dean of Rochester. Sixth Edition. Crown 4to. price 36s.

A **Lexicon, Greek and English,** abridged from LIDDELL and SCOTT'S *Greek-English Lexicon.* Twelfth Edition. Square 12mo. 7s. 6d.

A **SANSKRIT-ENGLISH DICTIONARY,** the Sanskrit words printed both in the original Devanagari and in Roman Letters. Compiled by T. BENFEY, Prof. in the Univ. of Göttingen. 8vo. 52s. 6d.

WALKER'S PRONOUNCING DICTIONARY of the **ENGLISH LANGUAGE.** Thoroughly revised Editions, by B. H. SMART. 8vo. 12s. 16mo. 6s.

A **PRACTICAL DICTIONARY** of the **FRENCH** and **ENGLISH LANGUAGES.** By L. CONTANSEAU. Fourteenth Edition. Post 8vo. 10s. 6d.

Contanseau's Pocket Dictionary, French and English, abridged from the above by the Author. New Edition, revised. Square 18mo. 3s. 6d.

NEW PRACTICAL DICTIONARY of the GERMAN LANGUAGE; German-English and English-German. By the Rev. W. L. BLACKLEY, M.A. and Dr. CARL MARTIN FRIEDLÄNDER. Post 8vo. 7s. 6d.

The **MASTERY of LANGUAGES;** or, the Art of Speaking Foreign Tongues Idiomatically. By THOMAS PRENDERGAST, late of the Civil Service at Madras. Second Edition. 8vo. 6s.

Miscellaneous Works and *Popular Metaphysics.*

The **ESSAYS** and **CONTRIBUTIONS** of A. K. H. B., Author of 'The Recreations of a Country Parson.' Uniform Editions:—

Recreations of a Country Parson. By A. K. H. B. FIRST and SECOND SERIES, crown 8vo. 3s. 6d. each.

The **COMMON-PLACE PHILOSOPHER in TOWN and COUNTRY.** By A. K. H. B. Crown 8vo. price 3s. 6d.

Leisure Hours in Town; Essays Consolatory, Æsthetical, Moral, Social, and Domestic. By A. K. H. B. Crown 8vo. 3s. 6d.

The Autumn Holidays of a Country Parson; Essays contributed to *Fraser's Magazine* and to *Good Words*. By A.K.H.B. Crown 8vo. 3s. 6d.

The Graver Thoughts of a Country Parson. By A. K. H. B. FIRST and SECOND SERIES, crown 8vo. 3s. 6d. each.

Critical Essays of a Country Parson, selected from Essays contributed to *Fraser's Magazine*. By A. K. H. B. Crown 8vo. 3s. 6d.

Sunday Afternoons at the Parish Church of a Scottish University City. By A. K. H. B. Crown 8vo. 3s. 6d.

Lessons of Middle Age; with some Account of various Cities and Men. By A. K. H. B. Crown 8vo. 3s. 6d.

Counsel and Comfort spoken from a City Pulpit. By A. K. H. B. Crown 8vo. price 3s. 6d.

Changed Aspects of Unchanged Truths; Memorials of St. Andrews Sundays. By A. K. H.B. Crown 8vo. 3s. 6d.

Present-day Thoughts; Memorials of St. Andrews Sundays. By A. K. H. B. Crown 8vo. 3s. 6d.

SHORT STUDIES on GREAT SUBJECTS. By JAMES ANTHONY FROUDE, M.A. late Fellow of Exeter Coll. Oxford. Third Edition. 8vo. 12s.

LORD MACAULAY'S MISCELLANEOUS WRITINGS:—
  LIBRARY EDITION. 2 vols. 8vo. Portrait, 21s.
  PEOPLE'S EDITION. 1 vol. crown 8vo. 4s. 6d.

The REV. SYDNEY SMITH'S MISCELLANEOUS WORKS; including his Contributions to the *Edinburgh Review*. Crown 8vo. 6s.

The Wit and Wisdom of the Rev. Sydney Smith: a Selection of the most memorable Passages in his Writings and Conversation. 16mo. 3s. 6d.

TRACES of HISTORY in the NAMES of PLACES; with a Vocabulary of the Roots out of which Names of Places in England and Wales are formed. By FLAVELL EDMUNDS. Crown 8vo. 7s. 6d.

The ECLIPSE of FAITH; or, a Visit to a Religious Sceptic. By HENRY ROGERS. Twelfth Edition. Fcp. 5s.

Defence of the Eclipse of Faith, by its Author; a rejoinder to Dr. Newman's *Reply*. Third Edition. Fcp. 3s. 6d.

Selections from the Correspondence of R. E. H. Greyson. By the same Author. Third Edition. Crown 8vo. 7s. 6d.

FAMILIES of SPEECH, Four Lectures delivered at the Royal Institution of Great Britain. By the Rev. F. W. FARRAR, M.A. F.R.S. late Fellow of Trinity College, Cambridge. Post 8vo. with Two Maps, 5s. 6d.

CHIPS from a GERMAN WORKSHOP; being Essays on the Science of Religion, and on Mythology, Traditions, and Customs. By MAX MÜLLER, M.A. &c. Foreign Member of the French Institute. 3 vols. 8vo. £2.

ANALYSIS of the PHENOMENA of the HUMAN MIND. By JAMES MILL. A New Edition, with Notes, Illustrative and Critical, by ALEXANDER BAIN, ANDREW FINDLATER, and GEORGE GROTE. Edited, with additional Notes, by JOHN STUART MILL. 2 vols. 8vo. price 28s.

An **INTRODUCTION to MENTAL PHILOSOPHY,** on the Inductive Method. By J. D. MORELL, M.A. LL.D. 8vo. 12s.

ELEMENTS of PSYCHOLOGY, containing the Analysis of the Intellectual Powers. By the same Author. Post 8vo. 7s. 6d.

The **SECRET of HEGEL:** being the Hegelian System in Origin, Principle, Form, and Matter. By J. H. STIRLING. 2 vols. 8vo. 28s.

Sir **William Hamilton**; being the Philosophy of Perception: an Analysis. By the same Author. 8vo. 5s.

The **SENSES and the INTELLECT.** By ALEXANDER BAIN, M.D. Professor of Logic in the University of Aberdeen. Third Edition. 8vo. 15s.

The **EMOTIONS and the WILL.** By the same Author. Second Edition. 8vo. 15s.

On the **STUDY of CHARACTER,** including an Estimate of Phrenology. By the same Author. 8vo. 9s.

MENTAL and MORAL SCIENCE: a Compendium of Psychology and Ethics. By the same Author. Second Edition. Crown 8vo. 10s. 6d.

LOGIC, DEDUCTIVE and INDUCTIVE. By the same Author. In TWO PARTS, crown 8vo. 10s. 6d. Each Part may be had separately:—
PART I. *Deduction,* 4s. PART II. *Induction,* 6s. 6d.

TIME and SPACE; a Metaphysical Essay. By SHADWORTH H. HODGSON. (This work covers the whole ground of Speculative Philosophy.) 8vo. price 16s.

The **Theory of Practice;** an Ethical Inquiry. By the same Author. (This work, in conjunction with the foregoing, completes a system of Philosophy.) 2 vols. 8vo. price 24s.

STRONG AND FREE; or, First Steps towards Social Science. By the Author of 'My Life, and What shall I do with it?' 8vo. price 10s. 6d.

The **PHILOSOPHY of NECESSITY;** or, Natural Law as applicable to Mental, Moral, and Social Science. By CHARLES BRAY. Second Edition. 8vo. 9s.

The **Education of the Feelings and Affections.** By the same Author. Third Edition. 8vo. 3s. 6d.

On **Force, its Mental and Moral Correlates.** By the same Author. 8vo. 5s.

A **TREATISE on HUMAN NATURE;** being an Attempt to Introduce the Experimental Method of Reasoning into Moral Subjects. By DAVID HUME. Edited, with Notes, &c. by T. H. GREEN, Fellow, and T. H. GROSE, late Scholar, of Balliol College, Oxford. [*In the press.*

ESSAYS MORAL, POLITICAL, and LITERARY. By DAVID HUME. By the same Editors. [*In the press.*

Astronomy, Meteorology, Popular Geography, &c.

OUTLINES of ASTRONOMY. By Sir J. F. W. HERSCHEL, Bart. M.A. Tenth Edition, revised; with 9 Plates and many Woodcuts. 8vo. 18s.

The SUN; RULER, LIGHT, FIRE, and LIFE of the PLANETARY SYSTEM. By RICHARD A. PROCTOR, B.A. F.R.A.S. With 10 Plates (7 coloured) and 107 Figures on Wood. Crown 8vo. 14s.

OTHER WORLDS THAN OURS; the Plurality of Worlds Studied under the Light of Recent Scientific Researches. By the same Author. Second Edition, with 14 Illustrations. Crown 8vo. 10s. 6d.

SATURN and its SYSTEM. By the same Author. 8vo. with 14 Plates, 14s.

SCHALLEN'S SPECTRUM ANALYSIS, in its application to Terrestrial Substances and the Physical Constitution of the Heavenly Bodies. Translated by JANE and C. LASSELL; edited by W. HUGGINS, LL.D. F.R.S. Crown 8vo. with Illustrations. [*Nearly ready.*

CELESTIAL OBJECTS for COMMON TELESCOPES. By the Rev. T. W. WEBB, M.A. F.R.A.S. Second Edition, revised, with a large Map of the Moon, and several Woodcuts. 16mo. 7s. 6d.

NAVIGATION and NAUTICAL ASTRONOMY (Practical, Theoretical, Scientific) for the use of Students and Practical Men. By J. MERRIFIELD, F.R.A.S and H. EVERS. 8vo. 14s.

DOVE'S LAW of STORMS, considered in connexion with the Ordinary Movements of the Atmosphere. Translated by R. H. SCOTT, M.A. T.C.D. 8vo. 10s. 6d.

M'CULLOCH'S DICTIONARY, Geographical, Statistical, and Historical, of the various Countries, Places, and Principal Natural Objects in the World. New Edition, with the Statistical Information brought up to the latest returns by F. MARTIN. 4 vols. 8vo. with coloured Maps, £4 4s.

A GENERAL DICTIONARY of GEOGRAPHY, Descriptive, Physical, Statistical, and Historical: forming a complete Gazetteer of the World. By A. KEITH JOHNSTON, LL.D. F.R.G.S. Revised Edition. 8vo. 31s. 6d.

A MANUAL of GEOGRAPHY, Physical, Industrial, and Political. By W. HUGHES, F.R.G.S. With 6 Maps. Fcp. 7s. 6d.

The STATES of the RIVER PLATE: their Industries and Commerce. By WILFRID LATHAM, Buenos Ayres. Second Edition, revised. 8vo. 12s.

MAUNDER'S TREASURY of GEOGRAPHY, Physical, Historical, Descriptive, and Political. Edited by W. HUGHES, F.R.G.S. Revised Edition, with 7 Maps and 16 Plates. Fcp. 6s. cloth, or 9s. 6d. bound in calf.

Natural History and Popular Science.

ELEMENTARY TREATISE on PHYSICS, Experimental and Applied. Translated and edited from GANOT'S *Éléments de Physique* (with the Author's sanction) by E. ATKINSON, Ph.D. F.C.S. New Edition, revised and enlarged; with a Coloured Plate and 620 Woodcuts. Post 8vo. 15s.

The ELEMENTS of PHYSICS or NATURAL PHILOSOPHY. By NEIL ARNOTT, M.D. F.R.S. Physician Extraordinary to the Queen. Sixth Edition, rewritten and completed. Two Parts, 8vo. 21s.

SOUND: a Course of Eight Lectures delivered at the Royal Institution of Great Britain. By JOHN TYNDALL, LL.D. F.R.S. New Edition, crown 8vo. with Portrait of *M. Chladni* and 169 Woodcuts, price 9s.

HEAT a MODE of MOTION. By Professor JOHN TYNDALL, LL.D. F.R.S. Fourth Edition. Crown 8vo. with Woodcuts, 10s. 6d.

RESEARCHES on DIAMAGNETISM and MAGNE-CRYSTALLIC ACTION; including the Question of Diamagnetic Polarity. By the same Author. With 6 Plates and many Woodcuts. 8vo. price 14s.

PROFESSOR TYNDALL'S ESSAYS on the USE and LIMIT of the IMAGINATION in SCIENCE. Being the Second Edition, with Additions, of his Discourse on the Scientific Use of the Imagination. 8vo. 3s.

NOTES of a COURSE of SEVEN LECTURES on ELECTRICAL PHENOMENA and THEORIES, delivered at the Royal Institution, A.D. 1870. By Professor TYNDALL. Crown 8vo. 1s. sewed, or 1s. 6d. cloth.

NOTES of a COURSE of NINE LECTURES on LIGHT delivered at the Royal Institution, A.D. 1869. By the same Author. Crown 8vo. price 1s. sewed, or 1s. 6d. cloth.

LIGHT: Its Influence on Life and Health. By FORBES WINSLOW, M.D. D.C.L. Oxon. (Hon.). Fcp. 8vo. 6s.

A TREATISE on ELECTRICITY, in Theory and Practice. By A. DE LA RIVE, Prof. in the Academy of Geneva. Translated by C. V. WALKER, F.R.S. 3 vols. 8vo. with Woodcuts, £3 13s.

The BEGINNING: its When and its How. By MUNGO PONTON, F.R.S.E. Post 8vo. with very numerous Illustrations. [*Just ready.*]

The FORCES of the UNIVERSE. By GEORGE BERWICK, M.D. Post 8vo. 5s.

The CORRELATION of PHYSICAL FORCES. By W. R. GROVE, Q.C. V.P.R.S. Fifth Edition, revised, and followed by a Discourse on Continuity. 8vo. 10s. 6d. The *Discourse on Continuity*, separately, 2s. 6d.

MANUAL of GEOLOGY. By S. HAUGHTON, M.D. F.R.S. Revised Edition, with 66 Woodcuts. Fcp. 7s. 6d.

VAN DER HOEVEN'S HANDBOOK of ZOOLOGY. Translated from the Second Dutch Edition by the Rev. W. CLARK, M.D. F.R.S. 2 vols. 8vo. with 24 Plates of Figures, 60s.

Professor OWEN'S LECTURES on the COMPARATIVE ANATOMY and Physiology of the Invertebrate Animals. Second Edition, with 235 Woodcuts. 8vo. 21s.

The COMPARATIVE ANATOMY and PHYSIOLOGY of the VERTE- brate Animals. By RICHARD OWEN, F.R.S. D.C.L. With 1,472 Woodcuts. 3 vols. 8vo. £3 13s. 6d.

The ORIGIN of CIVILISATION and the PRIMITIVE CONDITION of MAN; Mental and Social Condition of Savages. By Sir JOHN LUBBOCK, Bart. M.P. F.R.S. Second Edition, with 25 Woodcuts. 8vo. price 16s.

The PRIMITIVE INHABITANTS of SCANDINAVIA: containing a Description of the Implements, Dwellings, Tombs, and Mode of Living of the Savages in the North of Europe during the Stone Age. By SVEN NILSSON. With 16 Plates of Figures and 3 Woodcuts. 8vo. 18s.

BIBLE ANIMALS; being a Description of every Living Creature mentioned in the Scriptures, from the Ape to the Coral. By the Rev. J. G. WOOD, M.A. F.L.S. With about 100 Vignettes on Wood, 8vo. 21s.

HOMES WITHOUT HANDS: a Description of the Habitations of Animals, classed according to their Principle of Construction. By Rev. J. G. WOOD, M.A. F.L.S. With about 140 Vignettes on Wood, 8vo. 21s.

A FAMILIAR HISTORY of BIRDS. By E. STANLEY, D.D. F.R.S. late Lord Bishop of Norwich. Seventh Edition, with Woodcuts. Fcp. 3s. 6d.

The HARMONIES of NATURE and UNITY of CREATION. By Dr. GEORGE HARTWIG. 8vo. with numerous Illustrations, 18s.

The SEA and its LIVING WONDERS. By the same Author. Third (English) Edition. 8vo. with many Illustrations, 21s.

The TROPICAL WORLD. By Dr. GEO. HARTWIG. With 8 Chromoxylographs and 172 Woodcuts. 8vo. 21s.

The POLAR WORLD; a Popular Description of Man and Nature in the Arctic and Antarctic Regions of the Globe. By Dr. GEORGE HARTWIG. With 8 Chromoxylographs, 3 Maps, and 85 Woodcuts. 8vo. 21s.

KIRBY and SPENCE'S INTRODUCTION to ENTOMOLOGY, or Elements of the Natural History of Insects. 7th Edition. Crown 8vo. 5s.

MAUNDER'S TREASURY of NATURAL HISTORY, or Popular Dictionary of Zoology. Revised and corrected by T. S. COBBOLD, M.D. Fcp. with 900 Woodcuts, 6s. cloth, or 9s. 6d. bound in calf.

The TREASURY of BOTANY, or Popular Dictionary of the Vegetable Kingdom: including a Glossary of Botanical Terms. Edited by J. LINDLEY, F.R.S. and T. MOORE, F.L.S. assisted by eminent Contributors. With 274 Woodcuts and 20 Steel Plates. Two Parts, fcp. 12s. cloth, or 19s. calf.

The ELEMENTS of BOTANY for FAMILIES and SCHOOLS. Tenth Edition, revised by THOMAS MOORE, F.L.S. Fcp. with 154 Woodcuts. 2s. 6d.

The ROSE AMATEUR'S GUIDE. By THOMAS RIVERS. Ninth Edition. Fcp. 4s.

The BRITISH FLORA; comprising the Phænogamous or Flowering Plants and the Ferns. By Sir W. J. HOOKER, K.H. and G. A. WALKER-ARNOTT, LL.D. 12mo. with 12 Plates, 14s.

LOUDON'S ENCYCLOPÆDIA of PLANTS; comprising the Specific Character, Description, Culture, History, &c. of all the Plants found in Great Britain. With upwards of 12,000 Woodcuts. 8vo. 42s.

MAUNDER'S SCIENTIFIC and LITERARY TREASURY. New Edition, thoroughly revised and in great part re-written, with above 1,000 new Articles, by J. Y. JOHNSON, Corr. M.Z.S. Fcp. 6s. cloth, or 9s. 6d. calf.

A DICTIONARY of SCIENCE, LITERATURE, and ART. Fourth Edition, re-edited by W. T. BRANDE (the original Author), and GEORGE W. COX, M.A. assisted by contributors of eminent Scientific and Literary Acquirements. 3 vols. medium 8vo. price 63s. cloth.

Chemistry, Medicine, Surgery, and the Allied Sciences.

A DICTIONARY of CHEMISTRY and the Allied Branches of other Sciences. By HENRY WATTS, F.R.S. assisted by eminent Contributors. Complete in 5 vols. medium 8vo. £7 3s.

ELEMENTS of CHEMISTRY, Theoretical and Practical. By W. ALLEN MILLER, M.D. late Prof. of Chemistry, King's Coll. London. Fourth Edition. 3 vols. 8vo. £3. PART I. CHEMICAL PHYSICS, 15s. PART II. INORGANIC CHEMISTRY, 21s. PART III. ORGANIC CHEMISTRY, 24s.

A MANUAL of CHEMISTRY, Descriptive and Theoretical. By WILLIAM ODLING, M.B. F.R.S. PART I. 8vo. 9s. PART II. *just ready.*

OUTLINES of CHEMISTRY; or, Brief Notes of Chemical Facts. By WILLIAM ODLING, M.B. F.R.S. Crown 8vo. 7s. 6d.

A Course of Practical Chemistry, for the use of Medical Students. By the same Author. New Edition, with 70 Woodcuts. Crown 8vo. 7s. 6d.

Lectures on Animal Chemistry, delivered at the Royal College of Physicians in 1865. By the same Author. Crown 8vo. 4s. 6d.

Lectures on the Chemical Changes of Carbon. Delivered at the Royal Institution of Great Britain. By the same Author. Crown 8vo. price 4s. 6d.

A TREATISE on MEDICAL ELECTRICITY, THEORETICAL and PRACTICAL; and its Use in the Treatment of Paralysis, Neuralgia, and other Diseases. By JULIUS ALTHAUS. M.D. &c. Second Edition, revised and partly re-written. Post 8vo. with Plate and 2 Woodcuts, price 15s.

The DIAGNOSIS, PATHOLOGY, and TREATMENT of DISEASES of Women; including the Diagnosis of Pregnancy. By GRAILY HEWITT, M.D. Second Edition, enlarged; with 116 Woodcut Illustrations. 8vo. 24s.

LECTURES on the DISEASES of INFANCY and CHILDHOOD. By CHARLES WEST, M.D. &c. Fifth Edition, revised and enlarged. 8vo. 16s.

A SYSTEM of SURGERY, Theoretical and Practical. In Treatises by Various Authors. Edited by T. HOLMES, M.A. &c. Surgeon and Lecturer on Surgery at St. George's Hospital, and Surgeon-in-Chief to the Metropolitan Police. Second Edition, thoroughly revised, with numerous Illustrations. 5 vols. 8vo. £5 5s.

The SURGICAL TREATMENT of CHILDREN'S DISEASES. By T. HOLMES, M.A. &c. late Surgeon to the Hospital for Sick Children. Second Edition, with 9 Plates and 112 Woodcuts. 8vo. 21s.

LECTURES on the PRINCIPLES and PRACTICE of PHYSIC. By Sir THOMAS WATSON, Bart. M.D. New Edition in the press.

LECTURES on SURGICAL PATHOLOGY. By JAMES PAGET, F.R.S. Third Edition, revised and re-edited by the Author and Professor W. TURNER, M.B. 8vo. with 131 Woodcuts, 21s.

COOPER'S DICTIONARY of PRACTICAL SURGERY and Encyclopædia of Surgical Science. New Edition, brought down to the present time. By S. A. LANE, Surgeon to St. Mary's Hospital, assisted by various Eminent Surgeons. VOL. II. 8vo. completing the work. [*In the press.*

On **CHRONIC BRONCHITIS**, especially as connected with **GOUT**, EMPHYSEMA, and DISEASES of the HEART. By E. HEADLAM GREENHOW, M.D. F.R.C.P. &c. 8vo. 7s. 6d.

The **CLIMATE** of the **SOUTH** of **FRANCE** as **SUITED** to **INVALIDS**; with Notices of Mediterranean and other Winter Stations. By C. T. WILLIAMS, M.A. M.D. Oxon. Assistant-Physician to the Hospital for Consumption at Brompton. Second Edition. Crown 8vo. 6s.

REPORTS on the **PROGRESS** of **PRACTICAL** and **SCIENTIFIC** MEDICINE in Different Parts of the World, from June 1868, to June 1869. Edited by HORACE DOBELL, M.D. assisted by numerous and distinguished Coadjutors. 8vo. 18s.

PULMONARY CONSUMPTION; its Nature, Treatment, and Duration exemplified by an Analysis of One Thousand Cases selected from upwards of Twenty Thousand. By C. J. B. WILLIAMS, M.D. F.R.S. and C. T. WILLIAMS, M.A. M.D. Oxon. [*Nearly ready.*

CLINICAL LECTURES on **DISEASES** of the **LIVER, JAUNDICE**, and ABDOMINAL DROPSY. By CHARLES MURCHISON, M.D. Post 8vo. with 25 Woodcuts, 10s. 6d.

ANATOMY, DESCRIPTIVE and **SURGICAL**. By HENRY GRAY, F.R.S. With about 400 Woodcuts from Dissections. Fifth Edition, by T. HOLMES, M.A. Cantab. with a new Introduction by the Editor. Royal 8vo. 28s.

CLINICAL NOTES on **DISEASES** of the **LARYNX**, investigated and treated with the assistance of the Laryngoscope. By W. MARCET, M.D. F.R.S. Crown 8vo. with 5 Lithographs, 6s.

OUTLINES of **PHYSIOLOGY**, Human and Comparative. By JOHN MARSHALL, F.R.C.S. Surgeon to the University College Hospital. 2 vols. crown 8vo. with 122 Woodcuts, 32s.

ESSAYS on **PHYSIOLOGICAL SUBJECTS**. By GILBERT W. CHILD, M.A. Second Edition, revised, with Woodcuts. Crown 8vo. 7s. 6d.

PHYSIOLOGICAL ANATOMY and **PHYSIOLOGY** of **MAN**. By the late R. B. TODD, M.D. F.R.S. and W. BOWMAN, F.R.S. of King's College. With numerous Illustrations. VOL. II. 8vo. 25s.

VOL. I. New Edition by Dr. LIONEL S. BEALE, F.R.S. in course of publication; PART I. with 8 Plates, 7s. 6d.

COPLAND'S DICTIONARY of **PRACTICAL MEDICINE**, abridged from the larger work and throughout brought down to the present State of Medical Science. 8vo. 36s.

REIMANN'S HANDBOOK of **ANILINE** and its **DERIVATIVES**; a Treatise on the Manufacture of Aniline and Aniline Colours. Edited by WILLIAM CROOKES, F.R.S. With 5 Woodcuts. 8vo. 10s. 6d.

On the **MANUFACTURE** of **BEET-ROOT SUGAR** in **ENGLAND** and IRELAND. By WILLIAM CROOKES, F.R.S. Crown 8vo. with 11 Woodcuts, 8s. 6d.

A **MANUAL** of **MATERIA MEDICA** and **THERAPEUTICS**, abridged from Dr. PEREIRA's *Elements* by F. J. FARRE, M.D. assisted by R. BENTLEY, M.R.C.S. and by R. WARINGTON, F.R.S. 8vo. with 90 Woodcuts, 21s.

THOMSON'S CONSPECTUS of the **BRITISH PHARMACOPŒIA**. 25th Edition, corrected by E. LLOYD BIRKETT, M.D. 18mo. price 6s.

The Fine Arts, and Illustrated Editions.

IN FAIRYLAND; Pictures from the Elf-World. By RICHARD DOYLE. With a Poem by W. ALLINGHAM. With Sixteen Plates, containing Thirty-six Designs printed in Colours. Folio, 31s. 6d.

LIFE of JOHN GIBSON, R.A. SCULPTOR. Edited by Lady EASTLAKE. 8vo. 10s. 6d.

The LORD'S PRAYER ILLUSTRATED by F. R. PICKERSGILL, R.A. and HENRY ALFORD, D.D. Dean of Canterbury. Imp. 4to. price 21s. cloth.

MATERIALS for a HISTORY of OIL PAINTING. By Sir CHARLES LOCKE EASTLAKE, sometime President of the Royal Academy. 2 vols. 8vo. price 30s.

HALF-HOUR LECTURES on the HISTORY and PRACTICE of the Fine and Ornamental Arts. By WILLIAM B. SCOTT. New Edition, revised by the Author; with 50 Woodcuts. Crown 8vo. 8s. 6d.

ALBERT DURER, HIS LIFE and WORKS; including Autobiographical Papers and Complete Catalogues. By WILLIAM B. SCOTT. With Six Etchings by the Author, and other Illustrations. 8vo. 16s.

SIX LECTURES on HARMONY, delivered at the Royal Institution of Great Britain in the Year 1867. By G. A. MACFARREN. With numerous engraved Musical Examples and Specimens. 8vo. 10s. 6d.

The CHORALE BOOK for ENGLAND: the Hymns translated by Miss C. WINKWORTH; the tunes arranged by Prof. W. S. BENNETT and OTTO GOLDSCHMIDT. Fcp. 4to. 12s. 6d.

The NEW TESTAMENT, illustrated with Wood Engravings after the Early Masters, chiefly of the Italian School. Crown 4to. 63s. cloth, gilt top; or £5 5s. elegantly bound in morocco.

LYRA GERMANICA; the Christian Year. Translated by CATHERINE WINKWORTH; with 125 Illustrations on Wood drawn by J. LEIGHTON, F.S.A. 4to. 21s.

LYRA GERMANICA; the Christian Life. Translated by CATHERINE WINKWORTH; with about 200 Woodcut Illustrations by J. LEIGHTON, F.S.A. and other Artists. 4to. 21s.

The LIFE of MAN SYMBOLISED by the MONTHS of the YEAR. Text selected by R. PIGOT; Illustrations on Wood from Original Designs by J. LEIGHTON, F.S.A. 4to. 42s.

CATS' and FARLIE'S MORAL EMBLEMS; with Aphorisms, Adages, and Proverbs of all Nations. 121 Illustrations on Wood by J. LEIGHTON, F.S.A. Text selected by R. PIGOT. Imperial 8vo. 31s. 6d.

SHAKSPEARE'S MIDSUMMER - NIGHT'S DREAM, illustrated with 24 Silhouettes or Shadow-Pictures by P. KONEWKA, engraved on Wood by A. VOGEL. Folio. 31s. 6d.

SACRED and LEGENDARY ART. By Mrs. JAMESON.

Legends of the Saints and Martyrs. Fifth Edition, with 19 Etchings and 187 Woodcuts. 2 vols. square crown 8vo. 31s. 6d.

Legends of the Monastic Orders. Third Edition, with 11 Etchings and 88 Woodcuts. 1 vol. square crown 8vo. 21s.

Legends of the Madonna. Third Edition, with 27 Etchings and 165 Woodcuts. 1 vol. square crown 8vo. 21s.

The History of Our Lord, with that of his Types and Precursors. Completed by Lady EASTLAKE. Revised Edition, with 31 Etchings and 281 Woodcuts. 2 vols. square crown 8vo. 42s.

The Useful Arts, Manufactures, &c.

HISTORY of the GOTHIC REVIVAL; an Attempt to shew how far the taste for Mediæval Architecture was retained in England during the last two centuries, and has been re-developed in the present. By CHARLES L. EASTLAKE, Architect. With many Illustrations. [*Nearly ready.*

GWILT'S ENCYCLOPÆDIA of ARCHITECTURE, with above 1,600 Engravings on Wood. Fifth Edition, revised and enlarged by WYATT PAPWORTH. 8vo. 52s. 6d.

A MANUAL of ARCHITECTURE: being a Concise History and Explanation of the principal Styles of European Architecture, Ancient, Mediæval, and Renaissance; with their chief variations, and a Glossary of Technical Terms. By THOMAS MITCHELL. Crown 8vo. with 150 Woodcuts, 10s. 6d.

ITALIAN SCULPTORS; being a History of Sculpture in Northern, Southern, and Eastern Italy. By C. C. PERKINS. With 30 Etchings and 13 Wood Engravings. Imperial 8vo. 42s.

TUSCAN SCULPTORS, their Lives, Works, and Times. With 45 Etchings and 28 Woodcuts from Original Drawings and Photographs. By the same Author. 2 vols. imperial 8vo. 63s.

HINTS on HOUSEHOLD TASTE in FURNITURE, UPHOLSTERY, and other Details. By CHARLES L. EASTLAKE, Architect. Second Edition, with about 90 Illustrations. Square crown 8vo. 18s.

The ENGINEER'S HANDBOOK; explaining the Principles which should guide the Young Engineer in the Construction of Machinery. By C. S. LOWNDES. Post 8vo. 5s.

PRINCIPLES of MECHANISM, designed for the Use of Students in the Universities, and for Engineering Students generally. By R. WILLIS, M.A. F.R.S. &c. Jacksonian Professor in the University of Cambridge. Second Edition, enlarged; with 374 Woodcuts. 8vo. 18s.

LATHES and TURNING, Simple, Mechanical, and ORNAMENTAL. By W. HENRY NORTHCOTT. With about 240 Illustrations on Steel and Wood. 8vo. 18s.

URE'S DICTIONARY of ARTS, MANUFACTURES, and MINES. Sixth Edition, chiefly rewritten and greatly enlarged by ROBERT HUNT, F.R.S. assisted by numerous Contributors eminent in Science and the Arts, and familiar with Manufactures. With above 2,000 Woodcuts. 3 vols. medium 8vo. price £4 14s. 6d.

HANDBOOK of PRACTICAL TELEGRAPHY, published with the sanction of the Chairman and Directors of the Electric and International Telegraph Company, and adopted by the Department of Telegraphs for India. By R. S. CULLEY. Third Edition. 8vo. 12s. 6d.

ENCYCLOPÆDIA of CIVIL ENGINEERING, Historical, Theoretical, and Practical. By E. CRESY, C.E. With above 3,000 Woodcuts. 8vo. 42s.

TREATISE on MILLS and MILLWORK. By Sir W. FAIRBAIRN, F.R.S. Second Edition, with 18 Plates and 322 Woodcuts. 2 vols. 8vo. 32s.

USEFUL INFORMATION for ENGINEERS. By the same Author. FIRST, SECOND, and THIRD SERIES, with many Plates and Woodcuts. 3 vols. crown 8vo. 10s. 6d. each.

c

The **APPLICATION of CAST and WROUGHT IRON** to Building Purposes. By Sir W. FAIRBAIRN, F.R.S. Fourth Edition, enlarged; with 6 Plates and 118 Woodcuts. 8vo. price 16s.

IRON SHIP BUILDING, its History and Progress, as comprised in a Series of Experimental Researches. By the same Author. With 4 Plates and 130 Woodcuts. 8vo. 18s.

A TREATISE on the STEAM ENGINE, in its various Applications to Mines, Mills, Steam Navigation, Railways and Agriculture. By J. BOURNE, C.E. Eighth Edition; with Portrait, 37 Plates, and 546 Woodcuts. 4to. 42s.

CATECHISM of the STEAM ENGINE, in its various Applications to Mines, Mills, Steam Navigation, Railways, and Agriculture. By the same Author. With 89 Woodcuts. Fcp. 6s.

HANDBOOK of the STEAM ENGINE. By the same Author, forming a KEY to the Catechism of the Steam Engine, with 67 Woodcuts. Fcp. 9s.

BOURNE'S RECENT IMPROVEMENTS in the STEAM ENGINE in its various applications to Mines, Mills, Steam Navigation, Railways, and Agriculture. Being a Supplement to the Author's 'Catechism of the Steam Engine.' By JOHN BOURNE, C.E. New Edition, including many New Examples; with 124 Woodcuts. Fcp. 8vo. 6s.

A TREATISE on the SCREW PROPELLER, SCREW VESSELS, and Screw Engines, as adapted for purposes of Peace and War; with Notices of other Methods of Propulsion, Tables of the Dimensions and Performance of Screw Steamers, and detailed Specifications of Ships and Engines. By J. BOURNE, C.E. New Edition, with 54 Plates and 287 Woodcuts. 4to. 63s.

EXAMPLES of MODERN STEAM, AIR, and GAS ENGINES of the most Approved Types, as employed for Pumping, for Driving Machinery, for Locomotion, and for Agriculture, minutely and practically described. By JOHN BOURNE, C.E. In course of publication in 24 Parts, price 2s. 6d. each, forming One volume 4to. with about 50 Plates and 400 Woodcuts.

A HISTORY of the MACHINE-WROUGHT HOSIERY and LACE Manufactures. By WILLIAM FELKIN, F.L.S. F.S.S. Royal 8vo. 21s.

PRACTICAL TREATISE on METALLURGY, adapted from the last German Edition of Professor KERL's *Metallurgy* by W. CROOKES, F.R.S. &c. and E. RÖHRIG, Ph.D. M.E. With 625 Woodcuts. 3 vols. 8vo. price £4 19s.

MITCHELL'S MANUAL of PRACTICAL ASSAYING. Third Edition, for the most part re-written, with all the recent Discoveries incorporated, by W. CROOKES, F.R.S. With 188 Woodcuts. 8vo. 28s.

The **ART of PERFUMERY**; the History and Theory of Odours, and the Methods of Extracting the Aromas of Plants. By Dr. PIESSE, F.C.S. Third Edition, with 53 Woodcuts. Crown 8vo. 10s. 6d.

Chemical, Natural, and Physical Magic, for Juveniles during the Holidays. By the same Author. Third Edition, with 38 Woodcuts. Fcp. 6s.

LOUDON'S ENCYCLOPÆDIA of AGRICULTURE: comprising the Laying-out, Improvement, and Management of Landed Property, and the Cultivation and Economy of the Productions of Agriculture. With 1,100 Woodcuts. 8vo. 21s.

Loudon's Encyclopædia of Gardening: comprising the Theory and Practice of Horticulture, Floriculture, Arboriculture, and Landscape Gardening. With 1,000 Woodcuts. 8vo. 21s.

BAYLDON'S ART of VALUING RENTS and TILLAGES, and Claims of Tenants upon Quitting Farms, both at Michaelmas and Lady-Day. Eighth Edition, revised by J. C. MORTON. 8vo. 10s. 6d.

Religious and *Moral Works.*

CONSIDERATIONS on the REVISION of the ENGLISH NEW TESTAMENT. By C. J. ELLICOTT, D.D. Lord Bishop of Gloucester and Bristol. Post 8vo. price 5s. 6d.

An EXPOSITION of the 39 ARTICLES, Historical and Doctrinal. By E. HAROLD BROWNE, D.D. Lord Bishop of Ely. Seventh Edit. 8vo. 16s.

The LIFE and EPISTLES of ST. PAUL. By the Rev. W. J. CONYBEARE, M.A., and the Very Rev. J. S. HOWSON, D.D. Dean of Chester:—

LIBRARY EDITION, with all the Original Illustrations, Maps, Landscapes on Steel, Woodcuts, &c. 2 vols. 4to. 48s.

INTERMEDIATE EDITION, with a Selection of Maps, Plates, and Woodcuts. 2 vols. square crown 8vo. 31s. 6d.

STUDENT'S EDITION, revised and condensed, with 46 Illustrations and Maps. 1 vol. crown 8vo. price 9s.

The VOYAGE and SHIPWRECK of ST. PAUL; with Dissertations on the Life and Writings of St. Luke and the Ships and Navigation of the Ancients. By JAMES SMITH, F.R.S. Third Edition. Crown 8vo. 10s. 6d.

A CRITICAL and GRAMMATICAL COMMENTARY on ST. PAUL'S Epistles. By C. J. ELLICOTT, D.D. Lord Bishop of Gloucester & Bristol. 8vo.

Galatians, Fourth Edition, 8s. 6d.

Ephesians, Fourth Edition, 8s. 6d.

Pastoral Epistles, Fourth Edition, 10s. 6d.

Philippians, Colossians, and Philemon, Third Edition, 10s. 6d.

Thessalonians, Third Edition, 7s. 6d.

HISTORICAL LECTURES on the LIFE of OUR LORD JESUS CHRIST: being the Hulsean Lectures for 1859. By C. J. ELLICOTT, D.D. Lord Bishop of Gloucester and Bristol. Fifth Edition. 8vo. price 12s.

EVIDENCE of the TRUTH of the CHRISTIAN RELIGION derived from the Literal Fulfilment of Prophecy. By ALEXANDER KEITH, D.D. 37th Edition, with numerous Plates, in square 8vo. 12s. 6d.; also the 39th Edition, in post 8vo. with 5 Plates, 6s.

History and Destiny of the World and Church, according to Scripture. By the same Author. Square 8vo. with 40 Illustrations, 10s.

An INTRODUCTION to the STUDY of the NEW TESTAMENT, Critical, Exegetical, and Theological. By the Rev. S. DAVIDSON, D.D. LL.D. 2 vols. 8vo. 30s.

HARTWELL HORNE'S INTRODUCTION to the CRITICAL STUDY and Knowledge of the Holy Scriptures, as last revised; with 4 Maps and 22 Woodcuts and Facsimiles. 4 vols. 8vo. 42s.

Horne's Compendious Introduction to the Study of the Bible. Re-edited by the Rev. JOHN AYRE, M.A. With Maps, &c. Post 8vo. 6s.

HISTORY of the KARAITE JEWS. By WILLIAM HARRIS RULE, D.D. Post 8vo. price 7s. 6d.

NEW WORKS PUBLISHED BY LONGMANS AND CO.

EWALD'S HISTORY of ISRAEL to the DEATH of MOSES. Translated from the German. Edited, with a Preface and an Appendix, by RUSSELL MARTINEAU, M.A. Second Edition. 2 vols. 8vo. 24s.

The HISTORY and LITERATURE of the ISRAELITES, according to the Old Testament and the Apocrypha. By C. DE ROTHSCHILD and A. DE ROTHSCHILD. 2 vols. post 8vo. with 2 Maps, price 12s. 6d.
VOL. II. *The Historical Books*, price 7s. 6d.
VOL. II. *The Prophetic and Poetical Writings*, price 5s.

The SEE of ROME in the MIDDLE AGES. By the Rev. OSWALD J. REICHEL, B.C.L. and M.A. 8vo. price 18s.

The EVIDENCE for the PAPACY, as derived from the Holy Scriptures and from Primitive Antiquity. By the Hon. COLIN LINDSAY. 8vo. price 12s. 6d.

The TREASURY of BIBLE KNOWLEDGE; being a Dictionary of the Books, Persons, Places, Events, and other matters of which mention is made in Holy Scripture. By Rev. J. AYRE, M.A. With Maps, 16 Plates, and numerous Woodcuts. Fcp. 8vo. price 6s. cloth, or 9s. 6d. neatly bound in calf.

The GREEK TESTAMENT; with Notes, Grammatical and Exegetical. By the Rev. W. WEBSTER, M.A. and the Rev. W. F. WILKINSON, M.A. 2 vols. 8vo. £2 4s.

EVERY DAY SCRIPTURE DIFFICULTIES explained and illustrated. By J. E. PRESCOTT, M.A. VOL. I. *Matthew* and *Mark*; VOL. II. *Luke* and *John*. 2 vols. 8vo. 9s. each.

The PENTATEUCH and BOOK of JOSHUA CRITICALLY EXAMINED. By the Right Rev. J. W. COLENSO, D.D. Lord Bishop of Natal. People's Edition, in 1 vol. crown 8vo. 6s. or in 5 Parts, 1s. each.

SIX SERMONS on the FOUR CARDINAL VIRTUES (Fortitude, Justice, Prudence, Temperance) in relation to the Public and Private Life of Catholics; with Preface and Appendices. By the Rev. ORBY SHIPLEY, M.A. Crown 8vo. with Frontispiece, price 7s. 6d.

The FORMATION of CHRISTENDOM. By T. W. ALLIES. PARTS I. and II. 8vo. price 12s. each Part.

ENGLAND and CHRISTENDOM. By ARCHBISHOP MANNING, D.D. Post 8vo. price 10s. 6d.

CHRISTENDOM'S DIVISIONS, PART I., a Philosophical Sketch of the Divisions of the Christian Family in East and West. By EDMUND S. FFOULKES. Post 8vo. price 7s. 6d.

Christendom's Divisions, PART II. Greeks and Latins, being a History of their Dissensions and Overtures for Peace down to the Reformation. By the same Author. Post 8vo. 15s.

The HIDDEN WISDOM of CHRIST and the KEY of KNOWLEDGE; or, History of the Apocrypha. By ERNEST DE BUNSEN. 2 vols. 8vo. 28s.

The KEYS of ST. PETER; or, the House of Rechab, connected with the History of Symbolism and Idolatry. By the same Author. 8vo. 14s.

The TYPES of GENESIS, briefly considered as Revealing the Development of Human Nature. By ANDREW JUKES. Second Edition. Crown 8vo. 7s. 6d.

The Second Death and the Restitution of All Things, with some Preliminary Remarks on the Nature and Inspiration of Holy Scripture. By the same Author. Second Edition. Crown 8vo. 3s. 6d.

A VIEW of the SCRIPTURE REVELATIONS CONCERNING a FUTURE STATE. By RICHARD WHATELY, D.D. late Archbishop of Dublin. Ninth Edition. Fcp. 8vo. 5s.

The POWER of the SOUL over the BODY. By GEORGE MOORE, M.D. M.R.C.P.L. &c. Sixth Edition. Crown 8vo. 8s. 6d.

THOUGHTS for the AGE. By ELIZABETH M. SEWELL, Author of 'Amy Herbert' &c. Second Edition, revised. Fcp. 8vo. price 5s.

Passing Thoughts on Religion. By the same Author. Fcp. 8vo. 5s.

Self-Examination before Confirmation. By the same Author. 32mo. price 1s. 6d.

Readings for a Month Preparatory to Confirmation, from Writers of the Early and English Church. By the same Author. Fcp. 4s.

Readings for Every Day in Lent, compiled from the Writings of Bishop JEREMY TAYLOR. By the same Author. Fcp. 5s.

Preparation for the Holy Communion; the Devotions chiefly from the works of JEREMY TAYLOR. By the same Author. 32mo. 3s.

THOUGHTS for the HOLY WEEK for Young Persons. By the Author of 'Amy Herbert.' New Edition. Fcp. 8vo. 2s.

PRINCIPLES of EDUCATION Drawn from Nature and Revelation, and applied to Female Education in the Upper Classes. By the Author of 'Amy Herbert.' 2 vols. fcp. 12s. 6d.

The WIFE'S MANUAL; or, Prayers, Thoughts, and Songs on Several Occasions of a Matron's Life. By the Rev. W. CALVERT, M.A. Crown 8vo. price 10s. 6d.

SINGERS and SONGS of the CHURCH: being Biographical Sketches of the Hymn-Writers in all the principal Collections; with Notes on their Psalms and Hymns. By JOSIAH MILLER, M.A. Second Edition, enlarged. Post 8vo. price 10s. 6d.

LYRA GERMANICA, translated from the German by Miss C. WINKWORTH. FIRST SERIES, Hymns for the Sundays and Chief Festivals SECOND SERIES, the Christian Life. Fcp. 3s. 6d. each SERIES.

'SPIRITUAL SONGS' for the SUNDAYS and HOLIDAYS throughout the Year. By J. S. B. MONSELL, LL.D. Vicar of Egham and Rural Dean. Fourth Edition, Sixth Thousand. Fcp. 4s. 6d.

The BEATITUDES: Abasement before God; Sorrow for Sin; Meekness of Spirit; Desire for Holiness; Gentleness; Purity of Heart; the Peacemakers; Sufferings for Christ. By the same. Third Edition. Fcp. 3s. 6d.

His PRESENCE—not his MEMORY, 1855. By the same Author, in Memory of his SON. Sixth Edition. 16mo. 1s.

LYRA EUCHARISTICA; Hymns and Verses on the Holy Communion, Ancient and Modern: with other Poems. Edited by the Rev. ORBY SHIPLEY, M.A. Second Edition. Fcp. 5s.

Lyra Messianica; Hymns and Verses on the Life of Christ, Ancient and Modern; with other Poems. By the same Editor. Second Edition, altered and enlarged. Fcp. 5s.

Lyra Mystica; Hymns and Verses on Sacred Subjects, Ancient and Modern. By the same Editor. Fcp. 5s.

The LIFE of MARGARET MARY HALLAHAN, better known in the religious world by the name of Mother Margaret. By her RELIGIOUS CHILDREN. Second Edition. 8vo. with Portrait, 10s.

ENDEAVOURS after the CHRISTIAN LIFE: Discourses. By JAMES MARTINEAU. Fourth Edition, carefully revised. Post 8vo. 7s. 6d.

INVOCATION of SAINTS and ANGELS, for the use of Members of the English Church. Edited by the Rev. ORBY SHIPLEY. 24mo. 3s. 6d.

WHATELY'S INTRODUCTORY LESSONS on the CHRISTIAN Evidences. 18mo. 6d.

FOUR DISCOURSES of CHRYSOSTOM, chiefly on the Parable of the Rich Man and Lazarus. Translated by F. ALLEN, B.A. Crown 8vo. 3s. 6d.

BISHOP JEREMY TAYLOR'S ENTIRE WORKS. With Life by BISHOP HEBER. Revised and corrected by the Rev. C. P. EDEN, 10 vols. price £5 5s.

Travels, Voyages, &c.

The PLAYGROUND of EUROPE. By LESLIE STEPHEN, late President of the Alpine Club. Post 8vo. with Frontispiece. [Just ready.

CADORE; or, TITIAN'S COUNTRY. By JOSIAH GILBERT, one of the Authors of 'The Dolomite Mountains.' With Map, Facsimile, and 40 Illustrations. Imperial 8vo. 31s. 6d.

NARRATIVE of the EUPHRATES EXPEDITION carried on by Order of the British Government during the years 1835-1837. By General F. R. CHESNEY, F.R.S. With Maps, Plates, and Woodcuts. 8vo. 24s.

TRAVELS in the CENTRAL CAUCASUS and BASHAN. Including Visits to Ararat and Tabreez and Ascents of Kazbek and Elbruz. By D. W. FRESHFIELD. Square crown 8vo. with Maps, &c. 18s.

PICTURES in TYROL and Elsewhere. From a Family Sketch-Book. By the Authoress of 'A Voyage en Zigzag,' &c. Second Edition. Small 4to. with numerous Illustrations, 21s.

HOW WE SPENT the SUMMER; or, a Voyage en Zigzag in Switzerland and Tyrol with some Members of the ALPINE CLUB. From the Sketch-Book of one of the Party. In oblong 4to. with 300 Illustrations, 15s.

BEATEN TRACKS; or, Pen and Pencil Sketches in Italy. By the Authoress of 'A Voyage en Zigzag.' With 42 Plates, containing about 200 Sketches from Drawings made on the Spot. 8vo. 16s.

MAP of the CHAIN of MONT BLANC, from an actual Survey in 1863-1864. By A. ADAMS-REILLY, F.R.G.S. M.A.C. Published under the Authority of the Alpine Club. In Chromolithography on extra stout drawing-paper 28in. × 17in. price 10s. or mounted on canvas in a folding case, 12s. 6d.

WESTWARD by RAIL; the New Route to the East. By W. F. RAE. With Map shewing the Lines of Rail between the Atlantic and the Pacific, and Sections of the Railway. Post 8vo. price 10s. 6d.

HISTORY of DISCOVERY in our AUSTRALASIAN COLONIES, Australia, Tasmania, and New Zealand, from the Earliest Date to the Present Day. By WILLIAM HOWITT. 2 vols. 8vo. with 3 Maps, 20s.

The CAPITAL of the TYCOON; a Narrative of a Three Years' Residence in Japan. By Sir RUTHERFORD ALCOCK, K.C.B. 2 vols. 8vo. with numerous Illustrations, 42s.

ZIGZAGGING AMONGST DOLOMITES. By the Author of 'How we Spent the Summer, or a Voyage en Zigzag in Switzerland and Tyrol.' With upwards of 300 Illustrations by the Author. Oblong 4to. price 15s.

The DOLOMITE MOUNTAINS; Excursions through Tyrol, Carinthia, Carniola, and Friuli, 1861-1863. By J. GILBERT and G. C. CHURCHILL, F.R.G.S. With numerous Illustrations. Square crown 8vo. 21s.

GUIDE to the PYRENEES, for the use of Mountaineers. By CHARLES PACKE. 2nd Edition, with Map and Illustrations. Cr. 8vo. 7s. 6d.

The ALPINE GUIDE. By JOHN BALL, M.R.I.A. late President of the Alpine Club. Thoroughly Revised Editions, in Three Volumes, post 8vo. with Maps and other Illustrations:—

GUIDE to the WESTERN ALPS, including Mont Blanc, Monte Rosa, Zermatt, &c. Price 6s. 6d.

GUIDE to the CENTRAL ALPS, including all the Oberland District. Price 7s. 6d.

GUIDE to the EASTERN ALPS, price 10s. 6d.

Introduction on Alpine Travelling in General, and on the Geology of the Alps, price 1s. Each of the Three Volumes or Parts of the *Alpine Guide* may be had with this INTRODUCTION prefixed, price 1s. extra.

The HIGH ALPS WITHOUT GUIDES. By the Rev. A. G. GIRDLESTONE, M.A. late Demy in Natural Science, Magdalen College, Oxford. With Frontispiece and 2 Maps. Square crown 8vo. price 7s. 6d.

NARRATIVE of a SPRING TOUR in PORTUGAL. By A. C. SMITH, M.A. Ch. Ch. Oxon. Rector of Yatesbury. Post 8vo. price 6s. 6d.

ENGLAND to DELHI; a Narrative of Indian Travel. By JOHN MATHESON, Glasgow. With Map and 82 Woodcut Illustrations. 4to. 31s. 6d.

MEMORIALS of LONDON and LONDON LIFE in the 13th, 14th, and 15th Centuries; being a Series of Extracts, Local, Social, and Political, from the Archives of the City of London, A.D. 1276-1419. Selected, translated, and edited by H. T. RILEY, M.A. Royal 8vo. 21s.

COMMENTARIES on the HISTORY, CONSTITUTION, and CHARTERED FRANCHISES of the CITY of LONDON. By GEORGE NORTON, formerly one of the Common Pleaders of the City of London. Third Edition. 8vo. 14s.

The NORTHERN HEIGHTS of LONDON; or, Historical Associations of Hampstead, Highgate, Muswell Hill, Hornsey, and Islington. By WILLIAM HOWITT. With about 40 Woodcuts. Square crown 8vo. 21s.

VISITS to REMARKABLE PLACES: Old Halls, Battle-Fields, and Stones Illustrative of Striking Passages in English History and Poetry. By WILLIAM HOWITT. 2 vols. square crown 8vo. with Woodcuts, 25s.

The RURAL LIFE of ENGLAND. By the same Author. With Woodcuts by Bewick and Williams. Medium 8vo. 12s. 6d.

ROMA SOTTERRANEA; or, an Account of the Roman Catacombs, especially of the Cemetery of San Callisto. Compiled from the Works of Commendatore G. B. DE ROSSI by the Rev. J. S. NORTHCOTE, D.D. and the Rev. W. B. BROWNLOW. With numerous Illustrations. 8vo. 31s. 6d.

PILGRIMAGES in the PYRENEES and LANDES. By DENYS SHYNE LAWLOR. Crown 8vo. with Frontispiece and Vignette, price 15s.

Works of Fiction.

LOTHAIR. By the Right Hon. B. DISRAELI, M.P. Cabinet Edition (the Eighth), complete in One Volume, with a Portrait of the Author, and a New General Preface. Crown 8vo. price 6s.—By the Same Author, Cabinet Editions, revised, uniform with the above:—

CONINGSBY, 6s.
SYBIL, 6s.
TANCRED, 6s.
VENETIA, 6s.
HENRIETTA TEMPLE, 6s.
CONTARINI FLEMING AND RISE OF ISKANDER, 6s.

ALROY; IXION; THE INFERNAL MARRIAGE; AND POPANILLA Price 6s.
YOUNG DUKE AND COUNT ALARCOS, 6s.
VIVIAN GREY, 6s.

The MODERN NOVELIST'S LIBRARY. Each Work, in crown 8vo. complete in a Single Volume:—

MELVILLE'S GLADIATORS, 2s. boards; 2s. 6d. cloth.
——————— GOOD FOR NOTHING, 2s. boards; 2s. 6d. cloth.
——————— HOLMBY HOUSE, 2s. boards; 2s. 6d. cloth.
——————— INTERPRETER, 2s. boards; 2s. 6d. cloth.
——————— QUEEN'S MARIES, 2s. boards; 2s. 6d. cloth.
TROLLOPE'S WARDEN, 1s. 6d. boards; 2s. cloth.
——————— BARCHESTER TOWERS, 2s. boards; 2s. 6d. cloth.
BRAMLEY-MOORE'S SIX SISTERS of the VALLEYS, 2s. boards; 2s. 6d. cloth.

IERNE; a Tale. By W. STEUART TRENCH, Author of 'Realities of Irish Life.' 2 vols. post 8vo. [*Just ready.*

THREE WEDDINGS. By the Author of 'Dorothy,' 'De Cressy,' &c. Fcp. 8vo. price 5s.

STORIES and TALES by ELIZABETH M. SEWELL, Author of 'Amy Herbert,' uniform Edition, each *Story* or *Tale* complete in a single Volume:

AMY HERBERT, 2s. 6d.
GERTRUDE, 2s. 6d.
EARL'S DAUGHTER, 2s. 6d.
EXPERIENCE of LIFE, 2s. 6d.
CLEVE HALL, 3s. 6d.

IVORS, 3s. 6d.
KATHARINE ASHTON, 3s. 6d.
MARGARET PERCIVAL, 5s.
LANETON PARSONAGE, 4s. 6d.
URSULA, 4s. 6d.

A Glimpse of the World. By the Author of 'Amy Herbert.' Fcp. 7s. 6d.

The Journal of a Home Life. By the same Author. Post 8vo. 9s. 6d.

After Life; a Sequel to 'The Journal of a Home Life.' Price 10s. 6d.

UNCLE PETER'S FAIRY TALE for the NINETEENTH CENTURY. Edited by E. M. SEWELL, Author of 'Amy Herbert,' &c. Fcp. 8vo. 7s. 6d.

THE GIANT; A Witch's Story for English Boys. By the same Author and Editor. Fcp. 8vo. price 5s.

WONDERFUL STORIES from NORWAY, SWEDEN, and ICELAND. Adapted and arranged by JULIA GODDARD. With an Introductory Essay by the Rev. G. W. COX, M.A. and Six Woodcut Illustrations from Designs by W. J. Weigand. Square post 8vo. 6s.

VIKRAM and the VAMPIRE; or, Tales of Hindu Devilry. Adapted by RICHARD F. BURTON, F.R.G.S. &c. With 33 Illustrations by Ernest Griset. Crown 8vo. 9s.

A VISIT to MY DISCONTENTED COUSIN. Reprinted, with some Additions, from *Fraser's Magazine.* Crown 8vo. price 7s. 6d.

BECKER'S GALLUS; or, Roman Scenes of the Time of Augustus: with Notes and Excursuses. New Edition. Post 8vo. 7s. 6d.

BECKER'S CHARICLES; a Tale illustrative of Private Life among the Ancient Greeks: with Notes and Excursuses. New Edition. Post 8vo. 7s. 6d.

NOVELS and TALES by G. J. WHYTE MELVILLE :—
- *The* GLADIATORS, 5s.
- DIGBY GRAND, 5s.
- KATE COVENTRY, 5s.
- GENERAL BOUNCE, 5s.
- HOLMBY HOUSE, 5s.
- GOOD *for* NOTHING, 6s.
- The QUEEN'S MARIES, 6s.
- The INTERPRETER, 5s.

TALES of ANCIENT GREECE. By GEORGE W. COX, M.A. late Scholar of Trin. Coll. Oxon. Being a Collective Edition of the Author's Classical Stories and Tales, complete in One Volume. Crown 8vo. 6s. 6d.

A MANUAL of MYTHOLOGY, in the form of Question and Answer. By the same Author. Fcp. 3s.

OUR CHILDREN'S STORY, by one of their Gossips. By the Author of 'Voyage en Zigzag,' 'Pictures in Tyrol,' &c. Small 4to. with Sixty Illustrations by the Author, price 10s. 6d.

Poetry and *The Drama.*

THOMAS MOORE'S POETICAL WORKS, the only Editions containing the Author's last Copyright Additions :—
- CABINET EDITION, 10 vols. fcp. 8vo. price 35s.
- SHAMROCK EDITION, crown 8vo. price 3s. 6d.
- RUBY EDITION, crown 8vo. with Portrait, price 6s.
- LIBRARY EDITION, medium 8vo. Portrait and Vignette, 14s.
- PEOPLE'S EDITION, square crown 8vo. with Portrait, &c. 10s. 6d.

MOORE'S IRISH MELODIES, Maclise's Edition, with 161 Steel Plates from Original Drawings. Super-royal 8vo. 31s. 6d.

Miniature Edition of Moore's Irish Melodies with Maclise's Designs (as above) reduced in Lithography. Imp. 16mo. 10s. 6d.

MOORE'S LALLA ROOKH. Tenniel's Edition, with 68 Wood Engravings from original Drawings and other Illustrations. Fcp. 4to. 21s.

SOUTHEY'S POETICAL WORKS, with the Author's last Corrections and copyright Additions. Library Edition, in 1 vol. medium 8vo. with Portrait and Vignette, 14s.

LAYS of ANCIENT ROME; with *Ivry* and the *Armada*. By the Right Hon. LORD MACAULAY. 16mo. 4s. 6d.

Lord Macaulay's Lays of Ancient Rome. With 90 Illustrations on Wood, from the Antique, from Drawings by G. SCHARF. Fcp. 4to. 21s.

Miniature Edition of Lord Macaulay's Lays of Ancient Rome, with the Illustrations (as above) reduced in Lithography. Imp. 16mo. 10s. 6d.

GOLDSMITH'S POETICAL WORKS, with Wood Engravings from Designs by Members of the ETCHING CLUB. Imperial 16mo. 7s. 6d.

POEMS OF BYGONE YEARS. Edited by the Author of 'Amy Herbert,' &c. Fcp. 8vo. price 5s.

POEMS. By JEAN INGELOW. Fifteenth Edition. Fcp. 8vo. 5s.

POEMS by Jean Ingelow. With nearly 100 Illustrations by Eminent Artists, engraved on Wood by the Brothers DALZIEL. Fcp. 4to. 21s.

MOPSA the FAIRY. By JEAN INGELOW. Pp. 256, with Eight Illustrations engraved on Wood. Fcp. 8vo. 6s.

A STORY of DOOM, and other Poems. By JEAN INGELOW. Third Edition. Fcp. 5s.

The STORY of SIR RICHARD WHITTINGTON, Thrice Lord Mayor of London, A.D. 1397, 1406-7, and 1419. Written in Verse and Illustrated by E. CARR. With Ornamental Borders &c. on Wood, and 11 Copper-Plates. Royal 4to. 21s.

WORKS by EDWARD YARDLEY:—
    FANTASTIC STORIES. Fcp. 3s. 6d.
    MELUSINE AND OTHER POEMS. Fcp. 5s.
    HORACE'S ODES, translated into English Verse. Crown 8vo. 6s.
    SUPPLEMENTARY STORIES AND POEMS. Fcp. 3s. 6d.

GLAPHYRA, and OTHER POEMS By FRANCIS REYNOLDS, Author of 'Alice Rushton, and other Poems.' 16mo. price 5s.

BOWDLER'S FAMILY SHAKSPEARE, cheaper Genuine Editions: Medium 8vo. large type, with 36 Woodcuts, price 14s. Cabinet Edition, with the same ILLUSTRATIONS, 6 vols. fcp. 3s. 6d. each.

HORATII OPERA, Pocket Edition, with carefully corrected Text, Marginal References, and Introduction. Edited by the Rev. J. E. YONGE, M.A. Square 18mo. 4s. 6d.

HORATII OPERA. Library Edition, with Marginal References and English Notes. Edited by the Rev. J. E. YONGE. 8vo. 21s.

The ÆNEID of VIRGIL Translated into English Verse. By JOHN CONINGTON, M.A. New Edition. Crown 8vo. 9s.

ARUNDINES CAMI, sive Musarum Cantabrigiensium Lusus canori. Collegit atque edidit H. DRURY, M.A. Editio Sexta, curavit H. J. HODGSON, M.A. Crown 8vo. 7s. 6d.

HUNTING SONGS and MISCELLANEOUS VERSES. By R. E. EGERTON WARBURTON. Second Edition. Fcp. 8vo. 5s.

The SILVER STORE collected from Mediæval Christian and Jewish Mines. By the Rev. SABINE BARING-GOULD, M.A. Crown 8vo. 3s. 6d.

Rural Sports, &c.

ENCYCLOPÆDIA of RURAL SPORTS; a complete Account, Historical, Practical, and Descriptive, of Hunting, Shooting, Fishing, Racing, and all other Rural and Athletic Sports and Pastimes. By D. P. BLAINE. With above 600 Woodcuts (20 from Designs by JOHN LEECH). 8vo. 21s.

The DEAD SHOT, or Sportsman's Complete Guide; a Treatise on the Use of the Gun, Dog-breaking, Pigeon-shooting, &c. By MARKSMAN. Revised Edition. Fcp. 8vo. with Plates, 5s.

The FLY-FISHER'S ENTOMOLOGY. By ALFRED RONALDS. With coloured Representations of the Natural and Artificial Insect. Sixth Edition; with 20 coloured Plates. 8vo. 14s.

A BOOK on ANGLING; a complete Treatise on the Art of Angling in every branch. By FRANCIS FRANCIS. Second Edition, with Portrait and 15 other Plates, plain and coloured. Post 8vo. 15s.

The **BOOK** of the **ROACH**. By GREVILLE FENNELL, of 'The Field.' Fcp. 8vo. price 2s. 6d.

WILCOCKS'S SEA-FISHERMAN; comprising the Chief Methods of Hook and Line Fishing in the British and other Seas, a Glance at Nets, and Remarks on Boats and Boating. Second Edition, enlarged; with 80 Woodcuts. Post 8vo. 12s. 6d.

HORSES and STABLES. By Colonel F. FITZWYGRAM, XV. the King's Hussars. With Twenty-four Plates of Illustrations, containing very numerous Figures engraved on Wood. 8vo. 15s.

The **HORSE'S FOOT**, and **HOW to KEEP IT SOUND**. By W. MILES, Esq. Ninth Edition, with Illustrations. Imperial 8vo. 12s. 6d.

A PLAIN TREATISE on **HORSE-SHOEING**. By the same Author. Sixth Edition. Post 8vo. with Illustrations, 2s. 6d.

STABLES and STABLE-FITTINGS. By the same. Imp. 8vo. with 13 Plates, 15s.

REMARKS on **HORSES' TEETH**, addressed to Purchasers. By the same. Post 8vo. 1s. 6d.

ROBBINS'S CAVALRY CATECHISM, or Instructions on Cavalry Exercise and Field Movements, Brigade Movements, Out-post Duty, Cavalry supporting Artillery, Artillery attached to Cavalry. 12mo. 5s.

BLAINE'S VETERINARY ART; a Treatise on the Anatomy, Physiology, and Curative Treatment of the Diseases of the Horse, Neat Cattle and Sheep. Seventh Edition, revised and enlarged by C. STEEL, M.R.C.V.S.L. 8vo. with Plates and Woodcuts. 18s.

The **HORSE**: with a Treatise on Draught. By WILLIAM YOUATT. New Edition, revised and enlarged. 8vo. with numerous Woodcuts, 12s. 6d.

The **Dog**. By the same Author. 8vo. with numerous Woodcuts, 6s.

The **DOG** in **HEALTH and DISEASE**. By STONEHENGE. With 70 Wood Engravings. Square crown 8vo. 10s. 6d.

The **GREYHOUND**. By STONEHENGE. Revised Edition, with 24 Portraits of Greyhounds. Square crown 8vo. 10s. 6d.

The **OX**; his Diseases and their Treatment: with an Essay on Parturition in the Cow. By J. R. DOBSON. Crown 8vo. with Illustrations, 7s. 6d.

Commerce, Navigation, and Mercantile Affairs.

The **ELEMENTS of BANKING**. By HENRY DUNNING MACLEOD, M.A. Barrister-at-Law. Post 8vo. [*Nearly ready.*

The **THEORY and PRACTICE of BANKING**. By the same Author. Second Edition, entirely remodelled. 2 vols. 8vo. 30s.

A DICTIONARY, Practical, Theoretical, and Historical, of Commerce and Commercial Navigation. By J. R. M'CULLOCH, Esq. New and thoroughly revised Edition. 8vo. price 63s. cloth, or 70s. half-bd. in russia.

The **LAW of NATIONS** Considered as Independent Political Communities. By Sir TRAVERS TWISS, D.C.L. 2 vols. 8vo. 30s., or separately, PART I. *Peace*, 12s. PART II. *War*, 18s.

Works of *Utility* and *General Information*.

The CABINET LAWYER; a Popular Digest of the Laws of England, Civil, Criminal, and Constitutional. Twenty-fifth Edition, brought down to the close of the Parliamentary Session of 1870. Fcp. 10s. 6d.

PEWTNER'S COMPREHENSIVE SPECIFIER; A Guide to the Practical Specification of every kind of Building-Artificers' Work; with Forms of Building Conditions and Agreements, an Appendix, Foot-Notes, and a copious Index. Edited by W. YOUNG, Architect. Crown 8vo. price 6s.

The LAW RELATING to BENEFIT BUILDING SOCIETIES; with Practical Observations on the Act and all the Cases decided thereon; also a Form of Rules and Forms of Mortgages. By W. TIDD PRATT, Barrister. Second Edition. Fcp. 3s. 6d.

COLLIERIES and COLLIERS: a Handbook of the Law and Leading Cases relating thereto. By J. C. FOWLER, of the Inner Temple, Barrister, Stipendiary Magistrate for the District of Merthyr Tydfil and Aberdare. Second Edition. Fcp. 8vo. 7s. 6d.

The MATERNAL MANAGEMENT of CHILDREN in HEALTH and Disease. By THOMAS BULL, M.D. Fcp. 5s.

HINTS to MOTHERS on the MANAGEMENT of their HEALTH during the Period of Pregnancy and in the Lying-in Room. By the late THOMAS BULL, M.D. Fcp. 5s.

NOTES on HOSPITALS. By FLORENCE NIGHTINGALE. Third Edition, enlarged; with 13 Plans. Post 4to. 18s.

The PHILOSOPHY of HEALTH; or, an Exposition of the Physiological and Sanitary Conditions conducive to Human Longevity and Happiness. By SOUTHWOOD SMITH, M.D. Eleventh Edition, revised and enlarged; with 113 Woodcuts. 8vo. 7s. 6d.

CHESS OPENINGS. By F. W. LONGMAN, Balliol College, Oxford. Fcp. 8vo. 2s. 6d.

A PRACTICAL TREATISE on BREWING; with Formulæ for Public Brewers, and Instructions for Private Families. By W. BLACK. 8vo. 10s. 6d.

MODERN COOKERY for PRIVATE FAMILIES, reduced to a System of Easy Practice in a Series of carefully-tested Receipts. By ELIZA ACTON. Newly revised and enlarged Edition; with 8 Plates of Figures and 150 Woodcuts. Fcp. 6s.

COULTHART'S DECIMAL INTEREST TABLES at 24 Different Rates not exceeding 5 per Cent. Calculated for the use of Bankers. To which are added Commission Tables at One-Eighth and One-Fourth per Cent. 8vo. price 15s.

MAUNDER'S TREASURY of KNOWLEDGE and LIBRARY of Reference: comprising an English Dictionary and Grammar, Universal Gazetteer, Classical Dictionary, Chronology, Law Dictionary, a Synopsis of the Peerage, useful Tables, &c. Revised Edition. Fcp. 8vo. price 6s.

INDEX

Acton's Modern Cookery	28
Alcock's Residence in Japan	22
Allen's Four Discourses of Chrysostom	27
Allies on Formation of Christendom	20
Alpine Guide (The)	23
Althaus on Medical Electricity	14
Arnold's Manual of English Literature	7
Arnott's Elements of Physics	11
Arundines Cami	26
Autumn Holidays of a Country Parson	9
Ayre's Treasury of Bible Knowledge	20
Bacon's Essays, by Whately	6
———— Life and Letters, by Spedding	5
———— Works, edited by Spedding	6
Bain's Logic, Deductive and Inductive	10
———— Mental and Moral Science	10
———— on the Emotions and Will	10
———— on the Senses and Intellect	10
———— on the Study of Character	10
Ball's Alpine Guide	23
Baring's Staff College Essays	2
Bayldon's Rents and Tillages	18
Beaten Tracks	22
Becker's Charicles and Gallus	25
Benfey's Sanskrit Dictionary	8
Bernard on British Neutrality	1
Berwick's Forces of the Universe	12
Black's Treatise on Brewing	28
Blackley's Word-Gossip	7
———— German-English Dictionary	8
Blaine's Rural Sports	26
———— Veterinary Art	27
Bourne on Screw Propeller	18
Bourne's Catechism of the Steam Engine	18
———— Handbook of Steam Engine	18
———— Improvements in the Steam Engine	18
———— Treatise on the Steam Engine	18
———— Examples of Modern Engines	18
Bowdler's Family Shakspeare	26
Bramley-Moore's Six Sisters of the Valleys	24
Brande's Dictionary of Science, Literature, and Art	13
Bray's (C.) Education of the Feelings	10
———— Philosophy of Necessity	10
———— on Force	10
Browne's Exposition of the 39 Articles	19
Brunel's Life of Brunel	4
Buckle's History of Civilization	4
Bull's Hints to Mothers	24
———— Maternal Management of Children	24
Bunsen (Baron) Ancient Egypt	4
———— God in History	3
———— Memoirs	5
Bunsen (E. De) on Apocrypha	20
———— 's Keys of St. Peter	20
Burke's Vicissitudes of Families	5
Burton's Christian Church	4
———— Vikram and the Vampire	24
Cabinet Lawyer	28
Calvert's Wife's Manual	26
Carr's Sir R. Whittington	21
Cates's Biographical Dictionary	5
Cats' and Farlie's Moral Emblems	16
Changed Aspects of Unchanged Truths	9
Chesney's Euphrates Expedition	22
———— Indian Polity	3
———— Waterloo Campaign	2
———— and Reeve's Military Resources of Prussia and France, &c.	2
Child's Physiological Essays	15
Chorale Book for England	16
Clough's Lives from Plutarch	2
Colenso (Bishop) on Pentateuch	20
Commonplace Philosopher	9
Conington's Translation of the Æneid	26
Contanseau's French-English Dictionaries	8
Conybeare and Howson's St. Paul	19
Cotton's (Bishop) Life	5
Cooper's Surgical Dictionary	14
Copland's Dictionary of Practical Medicine	15
Coulthart's Decimal Interest Tables	28
Counsel and Comfort from a City Pulpit	9
Cox's Aryan Mythology	3
———— Manual of Mythology	25
———— Tale of the Great Persian War	2
———— Tales of Ancient Greece	25
Cresy's Encyclopædia of Civil Engineering	17
Critical Essays of a Country Parson	9
Crookes on Beet-Root Sugar	15
Culley's Handbook of Telegraphy	17
Cusack's History of Ireland	3
D'Aubigne's History of the Reformation in the time of Calvin	2
Davidson's Introduction to New Testament	19
Dead Shot (The), by Marksman	26
De La Rive's Treatise on Electricity	12
Denison's Vice-Regal Life	1
De Tocqueville's Democracy in America	2
Disraeli's Lothair	24
———— Novels and Tales	24
Dobell's Medical Reports	15
Dobson on the Ox	27
Dove on Storms	11
Doyle's Fairyland	16
Dyer's City of Rome	3
Eastlake's Hints on Household Taste	17

EASTLAKE'S History of Oil Painting 16
——— Gothic Revival 17
——— Life of Gibson 16
EDMUNDS'S Names of Places 9
Elements of Botany 13
ELLICOTT on the Revision of the English
New Testament 19
——'s Commentary on Ephesians 19
——— Commentary on Galatians 19
——————— Pastoral Epist. 19
——————— Philippians, &c. 19
——————— Thessalonians 19
——— Lectures on the Life of Christ.. 19
Essays and Contributions of A. K. H. B..... 8
EWALD'S History of Israel 20

FAIRBAIRN on Iron Shipbuilding 18
——————'s Applications of Iron 18
——————— Information for Engineers .. 17
——————— Mills and Millwork 17
FARADAY'S Life and Letters 4
FARRAR'S Families of Speech 9
——— Chapters on Language 7
FELKIN on Hosiery and Lace Manufactures 18
FENNELL'S Book of the Roach 27
FFOULKES'S Christendom's Divisions 20
FITZWYGRAM on Horses and Stables 27
FORBES'S Earls of Granard 5
FOWLER'S Collieries and Colliers 26
FRANCIS'S Fishing Book 26
FRESHFIELD'S Travels in the Caucasus 22
FROUDE'S History of England 1
——————— Short Studies on Great Subjects 9

GANOT'S Elementary Physics 11
GILBERT'S Cadore, or Titian's Country 22
GILBERT and CHURCHILL'S Dolomites 23
GIRDLESTONE'S High Alps without Guides 24
GLEDSTONE'S Life of WHITEFIELD 4
GODDARD'S Wonderful Stories 24
GOLDSMITH'S Poems, Illustrated 25
GOULD'S Silver Store 26
GRAHAM'S Book about Words 7
GRANT'S Home Politics 3
——— Ethics of Aristotle 6
Graver Thoughts of a Country Parson 9
GRAY'S Anatomy 15
GREENHOW on Bronchitis 15
GROVE on Correlation of Physical Forces .. 12
GURNEY'S Chapters of French History 2
GWILT'S Encyclopædia of Architecture 17

HAMPDEN'S (Bishop) Memorials 4
HARE on Election of Representatives 7
HARTWIG'S Harmonies of Nature 13
——————— Polar World 13
——————— Sea and its Living Wonders .. 13
——————— Tropical World 13
HAUGHTON'S Manual of Geology 12
HERSCHEL'S Outlines of Astronomy 11
HEWITT on Diseases of Women 14
HODGSON'S Theory of Practice 10
——————— Time and Space 10
HOLMES'S System of Surgery 14
——————— Surgical Diseases of Infancy ... 14
HOOKER'S British Flora 13
HORNE'S Introduction to the Scriptures.... 19
——————— Compendium of ditto 19
How we Spent the Summer 22
HOWITT'S Australian Discovery 22
——————— Northern Heights of London.... 23
——————— Rural Life of England......... 23

HOWITT'S Visits to Remarkable Places.... 23
HÜBNER'S Memoir of Sixtus V. 2
HUGHES'S (W.) Manual of Geography 11
HUME'S Essays 10
——— Treatise on Human Nature 10

IHNE'S Roman History 3
INGELOW'S Poems 25
——— Story of Doom 26
——— Mopsa 26

JAMESON'S Saints and Martyrs 16
——— Legends of the Madonna........ 16
——— Monastic Orders 16
JAMESON and EASTLAKE'S Saviour 16
JOHNSTON'S Geographical Dictionary 11
JUKES on Second Death 20
——— on Types of Genesis 21

KALISCH'S Commentary on the Bible 7
——— Hebrew Grammar 8
KEITH on Fulfilment of Prophecy 19
——— Destiny of the World 19
KERL'S Metallurgy 18
——— RÖHRIG 18
KIRBY and SPENCE'S Entomology 13

LATHAM'S English Dictionary 7
——— River Plate 11
LAWLOR'S Pilgrimages in the Pyrenees .. 23
LECKY'S History of European Morals 3
——— Rationalism 3
Leisure Hours in Town 9
Lessons of Middle Age 9
LEWES' History of Philosophy 3
LEWIS'S Letters 5
LIDDELL and SCOTT'S Two Lexicons 8
Life of Man Symbolised 16
Life of Margaret M. Hallahan 21
LINDLEY and MOORE'S Treasury of Botany 13
LINDSAY'S Evidence for the Papacy 20
LONGMAN'S Edward the Third 2
——— Lectures on the History of England 2
——— Chess Openings 28
Lord's Prayer Illustrated 16
LOUDON'S Agriculture 18
——— Gardening 18
——— Plants 13
LOWNDES'S Engineer's Handbook 13
LUBBOCK on Origin of Civilisation........ 12
Lyra Eucharistica 21
——— Germanica 16, 21
——— Messianica 21
——— Mystica 21

MACAULAY'S (Lord) Essays 3
——— History of England .. 1
——— Lays of Ancient Rome 25
——— Miscellaneous Writings 9
——— Speeches 7
——— Complete Works 1
MACFARREN'S Lectures on Harmony 16
MACLEOD'S Elements of Political Economy 7
——— Dictionary of Political Economy 7
——— Elements of Banking 27
——— Theory and Practice of Banking 27

McCULLOCH's Dictionary of Commerce.... 27
————————— Geographical Dictionary .. 11
MAGUIRE's Life of Father Mathew 5
————————— Pope Pius IX 5
MALET's Overthrow of the Germanic Confederation by Prussia..................... 2
MANNING's England and Christendom 20
MARCET on the Larynx 15
MARSHALL's Physiology..................... 15
MARSHMAN's Life of Havelock 5
————————— History of India 3
MARTINEAU's Christian Life 22
MASSINGBERD's History of the Reformation
MATHESON's England to Delhi 23
MAUNDER's Biographical Treasury........ 5
————————— Geographical Treasury 11
————————— Historical Treasury 4
————————— Scientific and Literary Treasury........................... 13
————————— Treasury of Knowledge...... 28
————————— Treasury of Natural History 13
MAY's Constitutional History of England.. 1
MELVILLE's Novels and Tales .... 24 & 25
Memoir of Bishop COTTON................... 4
MENDELSSOHN's Letters 5
MERIVALE's Fall of the Roman Republic.. 3
————————— Romans under the Empire 3
MERRIFIELD and EVER's Navigation 11
MILES on Horse's Foot and Horseshoeing .. 27
————————— Horses' Teeth and Stables 27
MILL (J.) on the Mind 10
MILL (J. S.) on Liberty 6
————————— on Representative Government 6
————————— on Utilitarianism............... 6
MILL's (J. S.) Dissertations and Discussions 7
————————— Political Economy 6
————————— System of Logic............. 6
————————— Hamilton's Philosophy...... 7
————————— Inaugural Address 7
————————— Subjection of Women........ 6
MILLER's Elements of Chemistry 14
————————— Hymn-Writers 21
MITCHELL's Manual of Architecture 17
————————— Manual of Assaying 18
MONSELL's Beatitudes..................... 21
————————— His Presence not his Memory 21
————————— 'Spiritual Songs'............. 21
MOORE's Irish Melodies 25
————————— Lalla Rookh 25
————————— Poetical Works 25
————————— Power of the Soul over the Body 21
MORELL's Elements of Psychology 10
————————— Mental Philosophy........... 10
MULLER's (MAX) Chips from a German
Workshop 19
————————— Lectures on the Science
of Language 7
————————— (K. O.) Literature of Ancient
Greece 3
MURCHISON on Liver Complaints........... 15
MURE's Language and Literature of Greece 2

New Testament, Illustrated Edition........ 16
NEWMAN's History of his Religious Opinions 5
NIGHTINGALE's Notes on Hospitals 28
NILSSON's Scandinavia 12
NORTHCOTE's Sanctuaries of the Madonna 23
NORTHCOTT's Lathes and Turning 17
NORTON's City of London 23

ODLING's Animal Chemistry 14
————————— Course of Practical Chemistry.. 14
————————— Manual of Chemistry............ 14
————————— Lectures on Carbon 14
————————— Outlines of Chemistry............ 14

O'FLANAGAN's Irish Chancellors ....
Our Children's Story....................... 25
OWEN's Lectures on the Invertebrate Animals 12
————————— Comparative Anatomy and Physiology of Vertebrate Animals 12

PACKE's Guide to the Pyrenees 23
PAGET's Lectures on Surgical Pathology .. 14
PEREIRA's Manual of Materia Medica 15
PERKIN's Italian and Tuscan Sculptors.... 17
PEWTNER's Comprehensive Specifier 28
Pictures in Tyrol 22
PIESSE's Art of Perfumery 18
————————— Natural Magic.................. 18
PONTON's Beginning....................... 12
PRATT's Law of Building Societies 28
PRENDERGAST's Mastery of Languages.... 8
PRESCOTT's Scripture Difficulties 20
Present-Day Thoughts..................... 9
PROCTOR on Plurality of Worlds 11
————————— Saturn and its System........ 11
————————— The Sun 11

RAE's Westward by Rail..................... 22
Recreations of a Country Parson.......... 8
REICHEL's See of Rome 20
REILY's Map of Mont Blanc................. 22
REIMANN on Aniline Dyes................. 15
REYNOLDS' Glaphyra, and other Poems .. 26
RILEY's Memorials of London.............. 23
RIVERS' Rose Amateur's Guide 13
ROBBIN's Cavalry Catechism 27
ROGER's Correspondence of Greyson 9
————————— Eclipse of Faith................ 9
————————— Defence of ditto............... 9
ROGET's English Words and Phrases...... 7
Roma Sotteranea........................... 24
RONALD's Fly-Fisher's Entomology 26
ROSE's Ignatius Loyola 2
ROTHSCHILD's Israelites.................... 23
ROWTON's Debater 7
RULE's Karaite Jews 19
RUSSELL's (Earl) Speeches and Despatches 1
————————— on Government and Constitution 1

SANDAR's Justinian's Institutes 6
SCHALLEN's Spectrum Analysis............. 11
SCOTT's Lectures on the Fine Arts 6
————————— Albert Durer 16
SEEBOHM's Oxford Reformers of 1498 2
SEWELL's After Life 21
————————— Amy Herbert 24
————————— Cleve Hall..................... 24
————————— Earl's Daughter................ 24
————————— Examination for Confirmation .. 21
————————— Experience of Life 24
————————— Gertrude 24
————————— Giant 24
————————— Glimpse of the World........... 24
————————— History of the Early Church.... 24
————————— Ivors 24
————————— Journal of a Home Life 24
————————— Katharine Ashton.............. 24
————————— Laneton Parsonage 21
————————— Margaret Percival 24
————————— Passing Thoughts on Religion .. 21
————————— Poems of Bygone Years'....... 25
————————— Preparations for Communion.... 21
————————— Principles of Education........ 21
————————— Readings for Confirmation 21
————————— Readings for Lent.............. 21
————————— Tales and Stories 24
————————— Thoughts for the Age 21
————————— Ursula 24
————————— Thoughts for the Holy Week.... 21

SHAKESPEARE'S Midsummer Night's Dream illustrated with Silhouettes	16
SHIPLEY'S Four Cardinal Virtues	20
—— Invocation of Saints	22
SHORT'S Church History	4
SMART'S WALKER'S Dictionary	8
SMITH'S (A. C.) Tour in Portugal	23
—— (Southwood) Philosophy of Health	28
—— (J.) Paul's Voyage and Shipwreck	19
—— (SYDNEY) Miscellaneous Works	9
—— Wit and Wisdom	9
—— Life and Letters	4
SOUTHEY'S Doctor	7
—— Poetical Works	25
STANLEY'S History of British Birds	13
STEBBING'S Analysis of MILL'S Logic	6
STEPHEN'S Ecclesiastical Biography	5
—— Playground of Europe	22
STIRLING'S Secret of Hegel	10
—— Sir WILLIAM HAMILTON	10
STONEHENGE on the Dog	27
—— on the Greyhound	27
STRICKLAND'S Tudor Princesses	5
—— Queens of England	5
Strong and Free	10
Sunday Afternoons at the Parish Church of a Scottish University City (St. Andrews)	9
TAYLOR'S History of India	3
—— (Jeremy) Works, edited by EDEN	22
THIRLWALL'S History of Greece	2
THOMPSON'S (Archbishop) Laws of Thought	7
—— (A. T.) Conspectus	15
Three Weddings	24
TODD (A.) on Parliamentary Government	1
TODD and BOWMAN'S Anatomy and Physiology of Man	15
TRENCH'S Ierne, a Tale	24
—— Realities of Irish Life	3
TROLLOPE'S Barchester Towers	24
—— Warden	24
TWISS'S Law of Nations	27
TYNDALL on Diamagnetism	12
—— Electricity	12
—— Heat	12
—— Imagination in Science	12
—— Sound	12

TYNDALL'S Faraday as a Discoverer	
—— Lectures on Light	
UNCLE PETER'S Fairy Tale	
URE'S Arts, Manufactures, and Mines	
VAN DER HOEVEN'S Handbook of Zoology	
Visit to my Discontented Cousin	
WARBURTON'S Hunting Songs	
WATSON'S Principles and Practice of Physic	
WATTS'S Dictionary of Chemistry	
WEBB'S Objects for Common Telescopes	
WEBSTER and WILKINSON'S Greek Testament	
WELLINGTON'S Life, by GLEIG	
WEST on Children's Diseases	
WHATELY'S English Synonymes	
—— Logic	
—— Rhetoric	
WHATELY on a Future State	
—— Truth of Christianity	
WHITE'S Latin-English Dictionaries	
WILCOCK'S Sea Fisherman	
WILLIAMS'S Aristotle's Ethics	
—— History of Wales	
WILLIAMS on Climate of South of France	
—— Consumption	
WILLIS'S Principles of Mechanism	
WINSLOW on Light	
WOOD'S Bible Animals	
—— Homes without Hands	
WOODWARD and CATES'S Encyclopædia	
YARDLEY'S Poetical Works	
YONGE'S English-Greek Lexicons	
—— Editions of Horace	
—— History of England	
YOUATT on the Dog	
—— on the Horse	
ZELLER'S Socrates	
—— Stoics, Epicureans, and Sceptics	
Zigzagging amongst Dolomites	

LONDON: PRINTED BY
SPOTTISWOODE AND CO., NEW-STREET SQUARE
AND PARLIAMENT STREET

www.ingramcontent.com/pod-product-compliance
Lightning Source LLC
Chambersburg PA
CBHW021841230426
43669CB00008B/1046